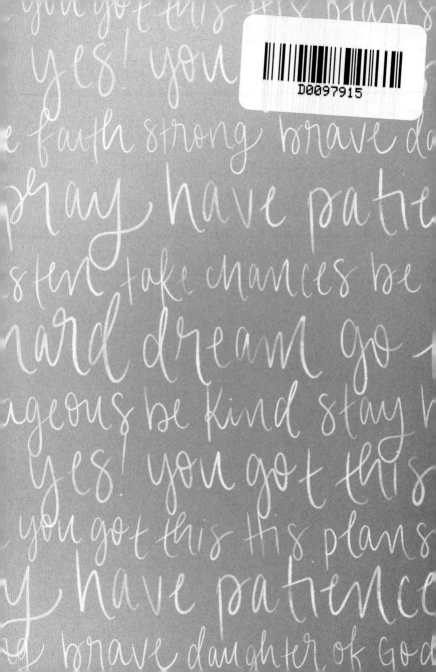

rong brave daughter of g
have patience su
take chances be you n
dream go for it
se kind stay humble
you got this work
his plans beautiful co
have patience su
strong brave daughter of g
am go for it pe
be you have faith st

TO:

FROM:

DATE:

HEY THERE! I'm Melissa Horvath. I'm a wife, a mom of two sweet little ones, and the founder, owner, and designer behind the home decor and gift company Sweet Water Decor. I love coffee, yoga pants, home renovation TV shows, looking up at the stars, jamming out to the same song on repeat, and following our Lord. Throughout my life, I've depended on God to get me through the good times and the not-so-fun times. A few years ago, God put it on my heart to write a book about purpose. He poured encouragement into my soul to share with the world... so I started to write, even before I knew where it would end up. And now, at this very moment, you are holding in your hands all the messages He poured into my heart to share with you. In each of these devotions, God wants you to deeply understand about who He is and how much He truly cares for you and your journey.

As you read through the following pages, know that I've prayed for you. I've prayed that your faith in Jesus will deepen and that you will realize all the special purposes and callings in your life. So sit back, pour a good cup of coffee (or tea!), and let's dive on in!

Your new friend, *Melissa*

*Keep on being encouraged + follow
along in my journey on instagram*

YOU GOT THIS

90 Devotions to Equip + Empower

hardworking women

MELISSA HORVATH

LIVE YOUR FAITH

You Got This: 90 Devotions to Equip + Empower Hardworking Women
Copyright © Melissa Horvath. All rights reserved.
First Edition, May 2021

Published by:

DaySpring

21154 Highway 16 East
Siloam Springs, AR 72761
dayspring.com

Written and hand lettered by: Melissa Horvath
Design by: Hannah Skelton

Printed in China
Prime: J4969
ISBN: 978-1-64454-988-9

CONTENTS

You are More 10

Living Like Jesus 12

Blessed versus Stressed. 14

Grace. 16

We are All Unique. 18

Her Success is Not Your Failure 20

Hearing from God 22

Waiting for His Message. 24

His Calling for You 26

Stuck 28

Nothing by Mistake 32

In a Hurry 34

Breaking the Mold 36

Victory 38

Finding Your Purpose 40

His Work isn't Done 42

Great Things Ahead 44

In the Storm. 46

Staying on the Right Path. 48

Silence the Fear 50

Unsettled 54

Sunk Cost. 56

Going the Other Way 58

God Sees What We Can't 60

Breakthrough. 62

What is Your "Why"? 64

Rest 66

Time Well Spent 68

God Provides. 70

Worth Isn't Measured 72

You Can Start Over Anytime. 76

Less is More 78

Working Smarter versus Harder 80

Chasing Slow 82

Pulling the Weeds 84

Saying No 86

Adding More to Our Plate 88

Regroup 90

How Do You See Yourself? 92

Jesus Has Overcome 94

Good Shepherd 98

Community versus Competition 100

Present Over Perfect 102

Fighting Your Battles 104

What Others Think 106

Work Hard and Stay Humble 108

Using the Best China 110

Allowed to be Happy! 112

Trusting God 114

Restoration. 116

Your Garden 120

The Tough Boss 122

Holding Strong 124

Honoring Work and Home 126

Doing Good 128

Praying for Your Work 130

For the Love of Money 132

God Never Changes 134

Second Place 136

Living Fearlessly 138

Once I Get 142

Life is Waiting for You 144

Own Path 146

Your Gifts 148

Giving Thanks 150

Living Water. 152

Grace and Mercy. 154

I Need You, Jesus. 156

Speak Truth 158

The Guide. 160

A Perfect World. 164

Listen Before Speaking. 166

Leading. 168

Be Strong and Speak Up. 170

Trust Fall. 172

Be Reminded 174

Serve Like Jesus. 176

Making a Difference 178

How Will You Sow? 180

No Time for This. 182

You Are the Salt 186

Standing Firm 188

Lifting Others Up 190

Being Authentic. 192

Taking Time Away 194

Filling the Void 196

Cheering on Others 198

His Timing is Perfect 200

Equipped. 202

You Got This 204

YOU ARE MORE

But to all who did receive him, who believed in his name,
he gave the right to become children of God.

JOHN 1:12 ESV

Sometimes when we wake up, it seems as if we're starting the same day all over again. We brush our teeth, get ourselves ready, eat breakfast, and start working. And if we don't watch it, we can even start feeling as if what we do defines who we are: "I am a mother. . . . I am a daughter. . . . I am a student. . . . I am a nurse. . . ." But what if we don't let these titles define us? What if we start realizing the truth—that we are much greater than the "titles" we hold. Think about it: our lives aren't defined by our titles but by what Jesus says we are. And He says that we are loved, cared for, and valued.

That's right—Jesus sees the beauty in you, even on your hard days when you yourself can't. You were made for many special purposes in life, and you can't let "titles" get in the way of that. When you feel as if you're not living up to your title, just look above. Your title as "child of God" is much greater than any other earthly title you can be given. He loves you beyond measure. He knows how many hairs are on your head. He knows what's best for you, even if you can't see it yet. Yes, He has given you many titles in life, but He doesn't want you to be defined by them. In fact, your entire identity can be found solely in His love for you!

YOU GOT THIS! *Take a moment to recall your younger years. What made your heart and soul feel alive? You are more than a wife, mom, worker, sister, or friend, and there's more to you than what you do every day. Remember the younger you? What did she love to do? What brought her joy? Free yourself from the many titles you have and the multitude of tasks on your plate today and do something that brings you joy. Release everything you have hanging over your head and take delight in being a child of God.*

LIVING LIKE JESUS

Judge not, that you be not judged. For with the judgment
you pronounce you will be judged, and with the measure
you use it will be measured to you. Why do you see the
speck that is in your brother's eye, but do not notice the
log that is in your own eye? Or how can you say to your
brother, 'Let me take the speck out of your eye,' when there
is the log in your own eye? You hypocrite, first take the log
out of your own eye, and then you will see clearly to take
the speck out of your brother's eye.

MATTHEW 7:1–5 ESV

It's in our human nature to judge others. We judge people for their actions, their choices, and sometimes even for their physical appearances. And even though we know that judging others only brings pain and conflict, we continue to make broad assumptions about people—sometimes with very little knowledge of their situation.

On the flip side, at one point or another, we've all been misjudged ourselves, leaving us feeling betrayed and hurt and misunderstood.

Let's take a look at how Jesus judged others. He washed the feet of people who were highly condemned for their actions, and He healed those judged and deemed unworthy by others. What would happen if we stopped our censure right away, turning our thoughts to prayer and love instead?

YOU GOT THIS! *Today, begin to turn your judgments into acceptance. Wouldn't you like to be accepted too? If we remember how Jesus treated others, we can begin to live like Him and do the same. No one is better than anyone else. If we take the first step and begin to love one another, messes and all, realizing that everyone is different, we can start living like Him.*

BLESSED VERSUS STRESSED

Do not be anxious about anything, but in everything by prayer and supplication with thanksgiving let your requests be made known to God.

PHILIPPIANS 4:6 ESV

Life is busy. Stress is real. And the mind knows just when to replay a slideshow filled with photos of past failures. Once that begins, we're reminded that we don't have time for the fun things we once did, and it doesn't take long to feel as if the world is crashing down around us. We've all been there.

Here's an idea: the next time we find ourselves stressed to the max with negative thoughts running amok, let's take a look around. Sometimes we forget all we truly do have. Even in times of stress, God provides. When negativity starts creeping in, turn stressful thoughts into remembering the blessings. Is work stressing you out? You have a job, and that's a blessing. Are the kids being crazy while you're trying to clean the house? You have little ones and a house, and those are blessings. Are you stressed because you can't see your friends? You have friends, and that's a blessing. Try looking at things outside of what's causing the stress and count the blessings around you. Be thankful for the clothes on your back or for having water to drink. Sometimes all it takes to stop the mental "failure slideshow" is to start thinking through all the things that have gone right, all the things for which you are grateful, and all the ways God has been faithful.

YOU GOT THIS!

What's something you're thankful for today? The next time a stressful thought enters your mind, recall the good the Lord has done for you—even the smallest things like the shoes on your feet or money in your pocket. Give your stresses to God and live in His grace. You'll end up finding that you can face each day, no matter how busy, with an inner peace of thankfulness.

GRACE

"My grace is sufficient for you, for my power is made perfect in weakness." Therefore I will boast all the more gladly of my weaknesses, so that the power of Christ may rest upon me.

II CORINTHIANS 12:9 ESV

Sometimes we are our own worst enemies. We tell ourselves we're not good enough, that we could lose a few pounds, or that our lives would be so much better if we didn't have x, y, or z. . . . Enter: grace. Think of the wonderful grace we receive from God. What if we started giving ourselves grace too? What if we allowed ourselves to be at peace with who we are? God made us in His image and how He wanted us to be. Maybe He made you with freckles or with long, brown hair . . . or maybe He made you a fast runner or someone who is better at cheering from the sidelines. We were all made to be who we are. Why are you hard on yourself when you were designed to be just who you are by the One Most High? When we start realizing whose we are, that's when grace can enter. When we are able to give ourselves grace, we can more easily offer it to others too.

YOU GOT THIS! *When have you wished you had received grace from another person? Think of a time recently when you could have offered grace to someone else. How do you think the situation would have been different if you had showed them love and grace instead? Practice grace today—not only with yourself but with others too. When you do this, you'll start to see yourself the way God sees you—beautiful, valuable, and one of a kind.*

WE ARE ALL UNIQUE

I praise you, for I am fearfully and wonderfully made.
Wonderful are your works; my soul knows it very well.

PSALM 139:14 ESV

Look down at your thumbprint. No one else will ever have the same print as you! God made you unique just the way you are. There are days when we don't feel like we're good enough, but isn't it wonderful to think that we were each uniquely created by the One Most High? He planned for you specifically even before you were born! He knew you would have many wonderful accomplishments, along with not-so-good times. He made you different from everyone else on purpose. Just think—He could have created a world where everyone looked and acted the same, but He didn't. We have all have been given different talents and special, unique characteristics. There was never anyone like you ever before, and there never will be again. God chose you to live now, in this time, in this season, and He has many great purposes for you. How awesome is that? As His child, you bring Him such joy. How are you using your individual characteristics and interests for good?

YOU GOT THIS!

Think about what you're good at or what gifts you've been given. How can you use those in your daily life, work life, or family life? What part of you can you share with the world—even right in your own home—to create happiness? When you are aligned with God, using the gifts He gave you to share His love, you'll find that life falls into place and that peace will reside in your heart.

HER SUCCESS IS NOT YOUR FAILURE

For am I now seeking the approval of man, or of God? Or am I trying to please man? If I were still trying to please man, I would not be a servant of Christ.

GALATIANS 1:10 ESV

I know there are days when the comparison game is strong. You may want what she has: "Her life looks a lot better than mine." . . . "Her kids behave." . . . "She has such a nice house, and I can never keep mine clean." . . . "She got the promotion; I didn't." . . . Whoever the she or shes are in your life, she is no better than you. She has her own struggles. Social media can make us believe that everyone has it good but us. Spoiler alert: social media isn't "real life." Most often, people share only the highlight reels of their lives. But in all actuality, behind the camera, her kid is screaming, her house is actually a mess, and so on. Just because she has something you feel you don't have, she's not any better than you.

On the flip side, let's take a moment to be honest with ourselves. How many of us have posted picture-perfect scenes on social media in an effort to make others jealous? Come on, ladies—who are you really seeking approval from? God wants us to use for good the talents and gifts He's graciously given us. God wants you to be you.

The next time you feel that the she in your life has it better than you or you start wishing you had what she has, try looking at everything you've got and count your blessings. Remember, everyone and every family has their own struggles, whether people know about them or not. Rest in the peace that God brings, knowing that He made you you!

YOU GOT THIS!

Instead of looking outwardly and comparing yourself to others, look inwardly and see what you need to celebrate! God made you unique— and just the way you are—for a reason. What are some ways you are you? What are some unique qualities you have or things you do best at? The next time you start comparing, what about turning it around? If you get down when measuring yourself against those on social media or other online sites, unfriend or unfollow those people. We don't want any negativity here! Feed your mind and your media only with things that bring you joy and celebrate you! You'll find yourself not living the comparison game and beginning to see the beauty inside you!

HEARING FROM GOD

My sheep hear my voice,
and I know them, and they follow me.

JOHN 10:27 ESV

Some of us know when God is talking to us, while others aren't so sure. God has many different ways of talking to us; sometimes He speaks through others or through a sign on the side of the road or through Scripture. God also guides us through His Holy Spirit, who dwells with us as our Comforter and Helper. It's so important to start listening and tuning in to the way He is trying to reach us. Jesus said, "But when the Father sends the Comforter instead of Me—and by the Comforter I mean the Holy Spirit—He will teach you much, as well as remind you of everything I myself have told you" (John 14:26 TLB).

You may sense the Holy Spirit guiding you during your morning quiet time or maybe even when you're taking a walk or doing the dishes. Remember, the Holy Spirit will never tell you to do anything that isn't of God's will. If you feel like you haven't heard from the Holy Spirit, pray for God to reveal Himself to you and to heighten your spiritual senses so you can see and hear from Him today. When He speaks, He will get your attention. Oftentimes you can feel His power and authority, especially when He calls you to do something that makes you feel uneasy or uncomfortable. We have to be okay with surrendering and knowing that His plans are much greater than anything we could think for ourselves.

YOU GOT THIS!

Have you heard direction from the Holy Spirit? How were you able to tell? Have you acted on His direction, or did you choose to go your own way? If you wish to be able to discern your inner voice from the Holy Spirit, pray for God to reveal Himself to you so that you can hear His plans for you. When you do this, you'll be tuned into God's guiding light throughout each and every day.

WAITING FOR
HIS MESSAGE

Let the word of Christ dwell in you richly, teaching and
admonishing one another in all wisdom, singing psalms and hymns
and spiritual songs, with thankfulness in your hearts to God.

COLOSSIANS 3:16 ESV

It's hard to wait, isn't it? I have two little ones, and they often have a hard time waiting, even if it's just for me to finish making lunch. We can feel the same way about our Father too. We want direction, and we want to be fed. But sometimes silence is His answer. He sees everything—our past, our present, and our future—while we can only see what is right in front of us. His plans are best, and they are greater than we could ever imagine. Aren't those good reasons to forget our agendas and be aligned with what He wants us to do? We should be okay in the waiting and trust that He wants us to be exactly where we are. When we wait for Him to move and then follow every step He lays before us, He will make our paths straight. It's when we get tired of waiting and start making moves on our own that we sometimes find ourselves worn out, discouraged, or lost. We need to trust Him. Listen for Him.

Maybe He is talking to you, but you don't feel like it's the right time to make a move—or maybe you feel that the task He's put before you is a little scary and way out of your comfort zone. Are you stuck in this tug-of-war waiting game? What would happen if you surrendered it all to God, and by all, I mean your time, energy, efforts—even your schedule, your life. If you laid it all at His feet, you would find that the time you are spending "waiting" on the Lord is never wasted. If He hasn't yet revealed His plans to you, He has you where you are for a reason. He may be growing you in your current position, or He may be preparing the way for your future. Whatever the case may be, you can know without a doubt that God is building a beautiful masterpiece. Think of a tapestry. If we looked at the back, we would see that all the wonderfully woven parts are connected—but it isn't until the tapestry is turned over that the beautiful picture is revealed. That's how God is working. He knows and sees all when we can't. It's when we surrender that we can feel at peace and trust in Him.

YOU GOT THIS!

When have you acted before hearing from God? Are you resisting anything that He's trying to tell you to do? Today and every day, try to be still to let the Holy Spirit speak to and guide you. If you feel as if you haven't heard from God, pray to have Him reveal Himself to you. It may take time, and that's okay! Just be open and wait for Him. If you do this, you might find that He opens just the right door for you at just the right time.

HIS CALLING FOR YOU

Therefore, my beloved, as you have always obeyed,
so now, not only as in my presence but much more in my
absence, work out your own salvation with fear and trembling,
for it is God who works in you, both to will and to work for his
good pleasure.

PHILIPPIANS 2:12–13 ESV

We love to make our own plans, don't we? We fill up our planners and set our schedules and give ourselves deadlines. Seriously, how many times have you heard the phrase, "By the age of thirty, I'm going to be. . ."? It's so hard for us planners to change course, but you know what's better than planning? The freedom of knowing that God has the sails.

In God's perfect timing, He'll reveal what's next for you. And when He starts to move, it may not be a huge transition; it may be one small change in your life that transforms everything. It could even be a quick nudge or reminder. We have to remember through it all that God knows what's best for us, better than we could ever imagine ourselves. By stepping away from what we feel is right for us, we can step toward trusting Him with our whole lives.

God has wonderful plans in store for you—and even more importantly, He has already equipped you for what He's calling you to do. Is there something He is calling you to that is a little out of your comfort zone? Is He asking you to step out of your "ordinary" and make a move that will ultimately cause a radical shift in your life? And are you scared? It's okay. Listen, I know it may seem easier to stay the course and keep going on with life "as is." But don't be afraid. When you say yes to God's plans, you're saying yes to a great adventure. He won't leave you. He'll walk you through it! All you have to do is surrender the perceived control you have over your life and allow Him to work it out for you. Isn't that a relief?

YOU GOT THIS! *Don't miss out! Take that step. Do it afraid! Soak up what He has for you. Enjoy these moments. If you're not happy in your situation, pray. God will reveal the next steps. And if you feel in your soul that something isn't right, maybe He's preparing you to move you on to what is next. Keep praying and seeking His voice, and He will unveil His plans for you. Hang in there!*

STUCK

Be still, and know that I am God.

PSALM 46:10 ESV

Whether it's a job or a relationship we are "stuck" in, we've all had that uneasy feeling cautioning or following us through our days—you know the one! It feels as if something isn't quite right, and we walk around with this annoying, unsettled sense as we go about our daily tasks, unable to shake the worry that we're missing something.

Have you tried praying and listening? Have you asked God what is stirring your heart? Have you asked Him what that edgy feeling is all about? Maybe you're in a waiting period, and if that's the case, stay the course! Don't let your lack of patience lead you to making your own plans. But if it's time to make a move, do it. You've got this!

The flesh is weak, but God is strong. In Genesis 3, Adam and Eve decided to take their lives into their own hands and disobeyed God. But in John 14:31 (NLT), Jesus gives us the perfect example of how obedience works. Jesus says, "I will do what the Father requires of me, so that the world will know that I love the Father." You see, our obedience is our response to God's love for us. And, if God is asking us to wait, being patient is part of letting the world know that we love our Father. It's all in God's timing, not ours.

If you're in a waiting period, try to be patient. Just because you've done the same thing for longer than you may have wanted to, it doesn't mean you have to do it forever. He will show you the way. If you try to take it in your own hands, it just won't work. But the best news is, you can wake up on any particular day and start again. There is always hope.

YOU GOT THIS!

What is making you miserable— or what in your life is calling for a revelation? Or a renewal? Maybe you're reading this and feel as if something is off in your marriage, a friendship, or a job. That job or husband or friend may not be ready yet. Don't settle. When you look back, it'll make sense. Just wait for His cue and go to what feels right in your heart and soul instead of the flesh. God is writing all our stories; in fact, even before you were born, your story was written. You were created by the One who created the universe—how wonderful is that? We're working for Him, not for us. Waiting is not wasting when you're waiting on the LORD. Enjoy the in-between times, soak up all you can, and learn what you can in that area. Don't always look for what's next; it'll be revealed to you in its own time, in God's timing.

she is
more
precious
than
rubies

—PROVERBS 3:15

NOTHING BY MISTAKE

For I know the plans I have for you, says the Lord.
They are plans for good and not for evil, to give you
a future and a hope.

JEREMIAH 29:11 TLB

Sometimes we wonder why certain people, situations, or jobs enter our lives. We have to remember that we only see what we see. God connects us to people who will help change us for the good. When we lose friends, relationships, or jobs we thought were gifts, God can use those situations to redirect our paths. He is always there for us, and His will for our lives is always more important than the losses we endure. Nothing He creates is by mistake. Nothing you've gone through wasn't allowed or meant to be. He is there through the pain, and He brings us through seasons of sorrow. He is there when we rejoice! He never leaves us, even when we feel like we're alone. He brings things and people in and out of our lives. He does it all for our good. It's hard to see the "why" when we are in a mess, but when we look back, we can see that it was used for His glory.

YOU GOT THIS!

Think of a time you were waiting for what you have now—maybe a new house, a friendship, or a certain relationship. Don't you wish you could have relaxed during that time versus being worried and or anxious for the day it would happen? That's what God wants from us: He wants us to give our waiting to Him and enjoy this beautiful life in the meantime. He already wrote your story before you were born, He knows what's best for you, and His story for you is better than you could ever imagine. Don't try to do it on your own—let Him work through you to make all things good.

IN A HURRY

For everything there is a season,
and a time for every matter under heaven.

ECCLESIASTES 3:1 ESV

Do you spend your life wanting what's next rather than being happy "in the now"? It's so easy to find ourselves wanting to hurry up at a red light or put our kids to bed in record time or finish a project as fast as possible. Often we get in a hurry just to wait. It's like waiting at a bus stop for one bus when we should have kept walking and enjoyed the scenery instead. Or maybe you're one who endlessly looks at the clock each day at work and can't wait for the day to end.

Does it help to know that there is meaning in every step of your journey, including the step you are on today? What if we stop wishing away time and start trusting the One who holds the universe together? We can trust in His perfect timing and know that His timing is better than we can ever imagine. He is paving the way and what's next for you even before you dream it up. And rest assured, even if you don't see it that way at the moment, someday you'll look back and see your "missed" opportunities as blessings in disguise. So instead of focusing on the next big thing, maybe it's time to look at the lessons you are learning right where you are—and maybe it's time to start enjoying the world around you instead of just wishing for the things ahead. He will put everything in line and in place. Don't get to the party early!

YOU GOT THIS!

What are you currently in a hurry for? What were some times in your past when you were in a hurry for something or someone? How would it have looked if you had just put your trust in the Lord and enjoyed that time instead?

BREAKING THE MOLD

Do not be conformed to this world,
but be transformed by the renewal of your mind,
that by testing you may discern what is the will of God,
what is good and acceptable and perfect.

ROMANS 12:2–3 ESV

Do you ever get upset when someone sits in your seat at lunch or parks in your spot at work? Jobs, houses, friends . . . we feel comfortable where we are, and change is hard to accept. We like to be the one in control of life. It makes us feel better, doesn't it? We watch the same shows on TV, listen to the same radio stations, and even order the same things at certain restaurants.

Have you ever had someone help you with your yard work? Their doing some of the work took part of the burden off you, and you were able to relax a bit. It is the same for what God wants from us. He wants us to cast our burdens on Him, and He wants to be the designer of our lives. We have to break the mold we've built around ourselves and allow change to happen. When we listen and obey God's calling for our lives, then we can begin something new. And here's a hint: God is already in control anyway. It's a whole lot easier to trust Him than be upset and fight for our own way. Accepting that God knows best will bring more blessings than you'd think!

YOU GOT THIS!

How have you built a mold around your life? How can you begin to surrender to Him for His control over your life? It's okay to feel uncomfortable when God is remolding us. Above all else, He is in control. It's hard to leave situations that are comfortable to pursue God's plans for us. But when He says to move, move. When he says to go, go. Don't fight the urge to stay in your mold; break through and experience the goodness He has in store for you.

VICTORY

But thanks be to God, who gives us the victory
through our Lord Jesus Christ.

I CORINTHIANS 15:57 ESV

In a sporting event, only one team wins and celebrates the victory; the other team heads home, disappointed. In our lifetime, we will get the chance to celebrate many victories, such as when we get that driver's license, nail that recipe, and even when we find that bargain at the store. . . . But who gets the credit?

When you have these victories (however minor they may seem), try to remember to thank God for eliminating the roadblocks, guiding you to success, and opening the right doors at the right time. God wants us to have victories in Him. Just as parents celebrate their children's victories—a first step, an A on a report card—God celebrates our victories too. When we get to the finish line and the crowd cheers, what's next? After a quick win and excitement, what happens after? When we strive to get ahead further and further . . . then what? Where is the ceiling? What are we striving for? What are we trying to obtain or accomplish? Is it a title, money, status, acceptance. . . ?

In today's world, it's so easy to lose focus on what brings

us true success and instead start striving for our own power, money, or status. It's always good to take a step back and realize that all we've been given (even that bargain at the grocery store) comes from God. While we get to celebrate it, the victories are not ours alone. They have and will always belong to God.

YOU GOT THIS!

What are you striving for in life? Take a look at your victories. What victory do you wish to accomplish? Power doesn't equal happiness, and neither does money. Isn't it better to work and act humbly? God longs to celebrate your victories with you, so remember to thank Him and give Him the credit He is due. He holds the universe together, and He paves the way for you. The next time you cross that finish line, think of how you got there. What steps did He prepare for you? And to whom will you give the credit?

FINDING YOUR PURPOSE

So we, though many, are one body in Christ, and individually members one of another. Having gifts that differ according to the grace given to us, let us use them.

ROMANS 12:5–6 ESV

We were put on this earth for many purposes. But for some reason, it's really easy to get stuck on thinking that our main purpose in life is based on our job or position or on our performance as a mom, daughter, sister, or friend. Is this you? Is your identity perhaps wrapped up in a title?

Try this: take a moment to write down what you enjoy doing. List all your hobbies, whether they be knitting or yoga or holding babies, or even writing or helping others. Dig deep. If you feel stuck in your job, think about the aspects of your position that spark joy. Why did you take your job in the first place? Think back to when you were younger: in which school subjects did you excel and love? Now look at your list and think about where your heart is going. We all have a purpose, and we were all made to be unique. How boring it would be if everyone were a doctor or a cook. There wouldn't be anyone exploring space or teaching young minds.

God delights in watching you enjoy the life He's designed for you. Yes, He gave you specific gifts, hobbies, and talents to help you fulfill His purpose for you. But He also gave you your unique characteristics so that you would enjoy the journey along the way. God may be calling you to share your unique gifts with the world right now. Or He may be calling you to wait where you are. If the latter is the case, ride the wave, soak up the sun, and find things to enjoy. Learn all you can in your current role, and let God help you dream about what's next. He is moving mountains for you even when you can't see it.

Spend some time exploring your talents, identifying what brings you joy, and listening to the little nudges God sends your heart. Then obey. And when you do that, get ready, because the adventure is just beginning.

YOU GOT THIS!

What do you really enjoy doing? What's keeping you from taking the next step toward something you were made to do, something that will bring you joy, or something that aligns with your God-given gifts? Remember, our purposes change throughout life, and we have many of them. In which areas of your life is your heart unsettled, and where do you sense He's moving you? Which areas of your life do you know you were called to be in, now and in the future?

HIS WORK ISN'T DONE

Trust in the LORD with all your heart,
and do not lean on your own understanding.
In all your ways acknowledge him,
and he will make straight your paths.

PROVERBS 3:5–6 ESV

God's work is never done in our lives. When we start one job and feel it'll be a lifetime career, God may have other plans. But don't be alarmed—He created us for so much more! In each season of life, our purpose molds, shifts, and reshapes. Your purpose is not defined by one thing or one moment. God is continuously writing our stories, and we have to be okay with a few plot twists. If you feel as if you have been forgotten, trust me, you have not. If you feel like you can't hear His direction, ask for clarity. He knows you, and He knows your heart. He has not forsaken you. Just because one door closes, it doesn't mean there's not another door waiting for you. Just as in nature, our lives have seasons too. There are times of drought and times of abundance. But rest assured, God is always working. There is a special purpose in each season, even when we can't see what it is. God knows what's coming up for you, and it's your part to trust Him with your past, present, and future.

YOU GOT THIS!

Remember, silence doesn't equal a lack of remembrance. Let God guide you in the waiting. Ask Him to give you an extra dose of patience and love. A table is being prepared for you, and even though it's hard to wait, it's so worth it. God's work has just begun.

GREAT THINGS AHEAD

Let all bitterness and wrath and anger and clamor and slander be
put away from you, along with all malice. Be kind to one another,
tenderhearted, forgiving one another, as God in Christ forgave you.

EPHESIANS 4:31-32 ESV

Negativity is a part of everyone's life. And it seems to show up more once a person starts pursuing God's purpose for their life. All of a sudden there's self-doubt and negative thoughts filling the mind, and it seems like everyone else is putting down those cherished hopes and dreams. Hurtful talk can come into our mind, and it takes away from God's plan for our lives for who we are and were made to be. Instead of letting the negativity take over our perspective, why not let it propel us further into God's plans for us? Instead of shrinking, let's not be swayed but instead wholeheartedly live out God's special plan for our lives, no matter how difficult it may be. When you find yourself in the downward spiral of negativity, remember this: you are not your circumstances. You can break through the mold and create a new path for your life and for your future. You are more than what you've been through . . . but those times helped shape you into who you are today. You can choose to break through the negativity and become your best self. You don't have to change who you are to grow into who God wants you to become. You were created for a purpose and not on accident, to glorify God and use your gifts for good. Just because you call yourself a Christian or believe in Jesus doesn't mean you'll have a flawless life or that you'll get everything you ever desired. It's through the broken times, even ones we didn't cause ourselves, that God works to make all things good. Sometimes we're born into someone else's brokenness, and we have no control over that. We have to look back at negative experiences and realize that they were all for a reason. Acknowledge them, but look ahead to the great things God has in store for you. You can wake up tomorrow and give all the negativity to God, and He will give you the grace you need to face anything that comes your way.

YOU GOT THIS! *What's something in your life that you want to give up to Him? What direction do you need to hear from Him? Forgive those in your past who have caused hurt or negativity and pray for them. Let God work and change your heart to look to the light and the goodness through Him.*

IN THE STORM

He replied, "You of little faith, why are you so afraid?"
Then He got up and rebuked the winds and the waves, and
it was completely calm.

MATTHEW 8:26 NIV

What is your favorite season? In Northeastern North America, we get to experience all the seasons. During the cold winter, the roads get icy and snow trucks with salt melt the ice and snow. As spring approaches, the storms bring rain, which washes away all the salt and dirt to pave a way for beautiful green grass and new life. Just as the earth goes through seasons, our lives have seasons as well. We go through storms, and the hardest ones make us cry out, "Why?" or "When?" But the good news is that God is there through it all. You are meant to be cleansed, just as the salt is cleared away by the rain. Your heart is renewed, strengthened, ready. You are not alone. We all go through the storms of life. Just think—if it never stormed or rained, how would we have food? Keep your face toward the sun and let the rays fill your soul and the Lord wash over you. Know that He is working to make all things good.

YOU GOT THIS! *When you're in a storm, remember, His timing is perfect. If we never went through the hard times, we wouldn't know when a good one comes. He prepares us for what's next. He is stronger and His plans are greater than any storm we face on earth. He knows your purpose and your story even before you were born. Every storm has its purpose, even when we can't see it.*

STAYING ON THE RIGHT PATH

One day he got into a boat with his disciples, and he said
to them, "Let us go across to the other side of the lake."
So they set out, and as they sailed he fell asleep. And a
windstorm came down on the lake, and they were filling
with water and were in danger. And they went and woke
him, saying, "Master, Master, we are perishing!" And
he awoke and rebuked the wind and the raging waves,
and they ceased, and there was a calm. He said to them,
"Where is your faith?" And they were afraid, and they
marveled, saying to one another, "Who then is this, that he
commands even winds and water, and they obey him?"

LUKE 8:22–25 ESV

Often we bring upon our own brokenness and suffering
and pain. We wonder why He has forsaken us, when all
along, it was God telling us to go down another path and
we decided to go our own way instead. Do you remember
being a child? I have a three-year-old, and he is starting to
tell me no. I say to him, "Jackson, don't jump off there!"
And you can guess what he does next—he jumps. "Ouch,
Mom! Kiss my boo-boo!" he cries. I respond, "Jackson, I

warned you not to jump, and you did it anyway." Just as my son tests me and wants to go his own way as I try to steer him the right way, God is doing the same for you. He gives you nudges and callings. Often we are scared to step away from the norm and what we're used to, or we try to decide what's best for us. Then, down the road, when things don't go as we'd planned, we look to Him—when He was telling us the right way all along.

YOU GOT THIS!

The good news is, He's always there for us. If you feel broken, scared, and down a road you can't turn around in, pray. Even if you make a wrong turn, He won't forsake you. Experiencing a failure doesn't mean that your life is a failure. Get back on the horse and keep riding!

SILENCE THE FEAR

Humble yourselves, therefore, under the mighty hand of God so that at the proper time he may exalt you, casting all your anxieties on him, because he cares for you.

I PETER 5:6–7 ESV

We let fear creep into our lives in so many ways. There's fear of the unknown, fear of losing, fear of failing, fear of change, fear of heights, spiders, snakes . . . the list goes on. And sometimes it feels like we have no control and we can't help but be scared. But here's the truth we must remember: Jesus is not fear. Jesus is love. He knows our hearts. And as our understanding of His perfect love increases, our fear decreases.

It's so easy to let our anxiety take control when we are waiting for God to reveal our next steps. Our thoughts spin, and we start asking questions such as, "Why am I stuck here?" or "Why can't I have the job that she has?" or "Why can't they see that I was meant for more than this?" In those moments, we can't let fear win . . . and we can't expect to have everything we want as soon as we want it, either—it's just not realistic. Even though we live in a "now" culture where we have access to food, information, and more than we would ever want or need, that's not how God works. Sometimes He asks us to wait, to have patience, and to do our best work in our current positions.

Fear makes us feel alone, when we are never alone. He is there with us in the waiting, guiding us and preparing us for what He has planned. We have to remember that it's not about us; it's about Him. When you fear, try to picture yourself in the presence of Jesus. Give your fears and worries to Him! He can silence the fear in our mind as we grow our confidence in Him. Learn to put all your trust in Him rather than in the situation. Remember, He's got this!

YOU GOT THIS!

When you start to fear, put on the armor of God. Ephesians 6:14–17 ESV says, "Stand therefore, having fastened on the belt of truth, and having put on the breastplate of righteousness, and, as shoes for your feet, having put on the readiness given by the gospel of peace. In all circumstances take up the shield of faith, with which you can extinguish all the flaming darts of the evil one; and take the helmet of salvation, and the sword of the Spirit, which is the word of God."

GOD'S
plan

OVER

mine

UNSETTLED

Search me, O God, and know my heart! Try me and know
my thoughts! And see if there be any grievous way in me,
and lead me in the way everlasting!

PSALM 139:23–24 ESV

Has your heart ever been unsettled? A lot of times we have something weighing on our souls that doesn't allow us to be happy. Maybe it's a project due at work or a broken relationship at home. Either way, we spend our days unsettled, walking around with a twinge of worry and concern in back of our minds (sometimes we're not even aware that it's there!). The next time that happens, why not search your heart for what's causing the pain and do some soul-cleansing?

Soul-cleansing starts with finding the cause of the unsettledness. Is it something you've left unsaid or a breakdown of communication in one of your most trusted relationships? Maybe it's a looming due date at work that you just don't think you can hit. Or maybe it's a job that's no longer serving you and you feel like there's no way out. Whatever it may be, identify the source and then give it to God, ask Him to work it out for you, and then watch everything fall into place. It's really a beautiful experience.

Often when we're unsettled, we aren't moving where God wants us to move. Maybe He's put it on your heart to do something and you've resisted. Search your heart and follow through with what He wants you to do. Have you felt anger or bitterness? When our minds are clear from pain, we can better hear His calling for us and what He wants from us. Trust me, He's always working to move you further in your faith journey. Take it to God and pray. You may not like His answer, but He knows what's best. He sees the past, the present, and the future. Listen to what He has to say, to change what's going on in your life, and you'll look back on this moment and think "Oh! That's what God was doing."

YOU GOT THIS!

When the walls are in front of us and there's no way out, prayer breaks through all walls. He will remove you from the situation if you answer His voice—His nudges to you. He won't physically remove you; that's up to you. It's also up to you to make the move, but it's best to obey.

SUNK COST

For still the vision awaits its appointed time;
it hastens to the end—it will not lie. If it seems slow,
wait for it; it will surely come; it will not delay.

HABAKKUK 2:3 ESV

We all look for signs and wonders from God to try to figure out our purpose in this life. We want to know now, in our timing. What we don't realize is that we're actually living out our purpose at this very moment. Callings don't happen overnight. Remember the old saying, "Rome wasn't built in a day"? Each day, God is working through us for His glory and to prepare us for our purpose.

Oftentimes we feel that our jobs should match up perfectly with what we studied in college or what we were trained to do or what our parents or others want us to do with our lives. But we get to make those decisions for ourselves. And better yet, you aren't making those decisions alone, because God has great plans for you.

Picking a college major is tough. How are we to know in our late teens and early twenties what we're to do for the rest of our lives? I remember walking back from a finance class with Jordan, one of my classmates, and he told me, "You know, I think I want to be a dentist." *A dentist? You're in your senior year of finance and you want to switch gears now? But you put in all this time to be a finance major.* All these things were going through my head. But he had a nudge, a calling.

We learned in economics class about a term called "sunk cost." It doesn't matter what we've done to this point; we've already done it or spent it. It's a sunk cost. We can move forward from there in a new direction, and it's better to change sooner than never. What if Jordan hadn't listened to God's plan for him and kept going on his path toward a finance degree? Today, he could be a really unhappy analyst, or he could be doing what he's doing today: helping others get a better smile and confidence while being a dentist, while fulfilling his God-given purpose. Kudos to you, Jordan! His story is a true testimony of listening and obeying. Just because we spend years doing something doesn't mean it has to define us for the rest of our lives.

YOU GOT THIS!

Did you ever stop to think that you are where you're at for a reason? Maybe God wants you to learn all you can there, or maybe the timing just has to be right for a move elsewhere. If you're in a relationship or a job and are not sure how to say good-bye but you know in your heart that it's just not right for you, pray and listen. God's timing is perfect. He knows our heart's desires, and He will make everything right in His time and for His glory.

GOING THE OTHER WAY

But I say, walk by the Spirit,
and you will not gratify the desires of the flesh.

GALATIANS 5:16 ESV

Are you a parent? If you're not, then maybe you remember doing this as a child: your mom or dad or someone older would tell you to do something, and you replied "No!" and did what you wanted instead. That's what it's like at my house with my three-year-old who is constantly not listening to me. When that happens, ahem, daily, it reminds me of how God must feel when He directs us and we respond, "No!" and then go off and do our own thing. Now, if you're a parent (even if you're a fur mama), you know how mad you get when your little one doesn't listen to you. You think and know what's best for them, and when they don't listen, they can even get a time-out. Have your parents ever said, "Fine. Then I guess we won't go to X Y Z since you didn't listen"?

Let's go back to the callings we have. Think about how many treasures you'll miss out on that God has stored for you when you say "No!" and go your own way. Think about all the places you won't get to go. How many times have you felt stuck and asked, "God, where are You?" Well, friends, I'm here to tell you, God is always there, and He wants what's best for you. He wants "far more than you could ever imagine or guess or request in your wildest dreams!"

(Ephesians 3:20 THE MESSAGE)—just as we want what's best for our kids and your parents wanted what was best for you. Parents try to keep their kids from harm, to direct them on the right path, and to teach them how to be good people. When we go our own way, we often stray from what our parents want for us and, in many cases, what God wants for us. So before taking a big step in life, sit quietly before Him and ask Him if that is the way. If the answer is "wait," don't be discouraged. He is working it all out, and it's going to be amazing. Just breathe.

YOU GOT THIS!

When you get those nudges in your soul to take a big step or go in a different direction, take a posture of obedience. What God is asking you to do may be way out of your comfort zone or perhaps you don't feel equipped to do what He's calling you to. Instead of having doubt, have trust in the One Most High. If He is calling you to do it and you don't move as you should, you'll miss all the wonderful things He has in store for you!

GOD SEES
WHAT WE CAN'T

He has made everything beautiful in its time. Also, he has put
eternity into man's heart, yet so that he cannot find out what God
has done from the beginning to the end.

ECCLESIASTES 3:11 ESV

God's timing is best. I remember having conversations with God about finding my husband. It seemed like every guy I dated or laid eyes on, I wondered, *Is it him? Is he "the one"?* I would say, "Okay, God, can I please meet my husband now? I'm done waiting. I am ready to get married." And then God would tell me that my husband wasn't quite ready for me yet. God would say that He was working through my future husband and if I were to meet him now, things wouldn't work out the way He had planned. And then I would say, "Okay, but how about my job? I really want to move up in the company, and I've worked so hard. Why won't my boss let me?" And God would respond by saying that He had other plans for me—plans outside of that company, which was why He was closing doors at my current job.

See the pattern here? We think we know what's best for us, but when we look back at our life and our purpose, we'll see that God was laying the groundwork for us. Currently we can only see what we know, but He sees the full picture, inside and out and all around. God not only sees your story but everyone else's too, as well as how they intertwine. If things aren't exactly going your way, don't get angry but be glad that He has a better way. That missed date, arriving late, a job that fell through . . . there was a reason for it (maybe even many reasons for it), so things could fall into place just right. What if He sees the good that we cannot? When He's ready and calls you to start or change something— even if it is out of character—go, do, and just obey. Those small steps of obedience lead to wonderful things ahead.

YOU GOT THIS!

What answers are you waiting on from God right now? Instead of thinking you've been forgotten, remember that He has your best interests in mind. Let go of the control and the plans you're making and start letting God take control of the sails. Say a prayer and let Him know how you feel, and then release the reins and let Him help the sails.

BREAKTHROUGH

Jesus then said to them, "Truly, truly, I say to you, it was not Moses who gave you the bread from heaven, but my Father gives you the true bread from heaven. For the bread of God is he who comes down from heaven and gives life to the world." They said to him, "Sir, give us this bread always." Jesus said to them, "I am the bread of life; whoever comes to me shall not hunger, and whoever believes in me shall never thirst."

JOHN 6:32–35 ESV

We have moments in our lives when we seek a breakthrough from above—when something in our lives needs to have a good change. Did you ever notice that when we come to God seeking a breakthrough in our lives, we tend to focus on what we need help with more than we focus on the One who can make it happen? God provides a way when we feel there is no other way—when it seems that all the doors and windows are closed. What we need to remember is that He is always working behind the scenes. God sees and thinks eternally, while we only have finite knowledge. Instead of merely wanting something to change in your life, seek the God who can make it all happen. Seek Him over all your wants and needs in life. Bread can waste away, but God's love is everlasting. We need Jesus more than our wants.

And when you receive breakthroughs in life, remember to look up! That beautiful moment came from a loving God who sees you and loves you. God knows what's best for you. He knows what you need, He knows the right timing, and He will work out situations for your good.

YOU GOT THIS! *What breakthrough in your life are you currently seeking? Recall a time when you called on God to make a change in your life. Did it happen? When you got answers, how did you feel about them? Were you mad that God's plans were different from yours? Or did you focus on what He did for you? The next time you see the work of God in your life, whether it's what you wanted or not, remember who holds you in His hands and has the best intentions for you.*

WHAT IS YOUR "WHY"?

*Having gifts that differ according to the grace
given to us, let us use them: if prophecy, in proportion to our
faith; if service, in our serving; the one who teaches, in his
teaching; the one who exhorts, in his exhortation; the one
who contributes, in generosity; the one who leads, with zeal;
the one who does acts of mercy, with cheerfulness.*

ROMANS 12:6–8 ESV

What are you striving for in life? Is it to satisfy your own desires or to live out your God-given purpose? Sometimes this question can be a reality check, especially when our plans don't align with God's. You are meant for so much more than your earthly desires! When we surrender our lives to His glory and His kingdom—when we release our own satisfaction and glory—only then can we start to be okay with the idea that what we hoped for wasn't meant to be ours.

He gave you wonderful and beautiful talents for you to put your unique stamp on the world and do what you were meant to do. If we all had the same job or the same duties, the world wouldn't work efficiently. Whether you are a stay-at-home mom, a full-time student, or a hardworking professional, remember that you are doing great work, the work the Creator of the universe called you to do. So when days get hard, remember, you're doing it for His glory, not your own.

YOU GOT THIS!

When you feel pushed to your limits, sit back and remember whose you are. He's equipped you to do what you're doing, even though you may feel like giving up some days. Look to the One above for strength. He wants you to stay the strong woman He's made you to be. Work hard, but remember the One who got you where you are today!

REST

*And on the seventh day God finished his work
that he had done, and he rested on the seventh day from all his
work that he had done.*

GENESIS 2:2 ESV

When you are juggling work, family, laundry, dinner, and an ever-growing to-do list, it's difficult to find time to rest. But the truth is that if you don't feel rested, if you never slow down, if you never stop to smell the roses, you will experience burnout. That's why we all need a "me" day once in a while to escape the noise, rest up, recharge, and truly put ourselves back together. What would happen if you just dropped it all and walked away for a few days? I know, I know, a few days is hard to do. A month-long getaway to Fiji is likely out of the question too . . . but what about an hour a day—an hour a day set aside for you to experience God's rest?

You could get up early while everyone else is asleep, read a book, exercise, or simply pour yourself a good cup of coffee and watch the sunrise. Or if evening is more your thing, maybe grab a cup of hot tea and watch the sun set or the stars shine. Maybe it's time to book that spa appointment, ask your husband for a date and get a sitter for the kids, take a personal day and plan a fun day for you and your kids, or do whatever brings your heart rest and fills your soul! Whatever you choose, just vow to get lost without getting lost while scrolling through social media. Try not to think of work, negativity, or anything else that creeps in. Ask God to take all the negative thoughts away and allow His peace to fill your mind instead.

It's easy to put ourselves last when there are so many things to do and so many people relying on us to do those things, but if we don't find time to refresh and renew our soul, we could end up feeling empty and mentally exhausted, devoid of motivation and beyond caring.

YOU GOT THIS!

Let's take inventory: How do you feel right now? Do you feel fulfilled? Do you feel renewed? Are you happy? If not, what would make you happy? We all need to step away from the roles we are in and take a minute to remember who we are and whose we are. While you're resting, don't forget to listen. It's often in these kinds of times when God speaks to us, when His nudges come and our purpose grows. Taking time away is not selfish; it's a necessary means for you to recharge and stay aligned with God's plan and purpose for your life.

TIME WELL SPENT

*Do not love the world or the things in the world. If anyone loves
the world, the love of the Father is not in him. For all that is in
the world—the desires of the flesh and the desires of the eyes and
pride of life—is not from the Father but is from the world. And
the world is passing away along with its desires, but whoever does
the will of God abides forever.*

I JOHN 2:15–17 ESV

As you look back on all the things you did today, what did you value most? Did you spend fifteen minutes getting the best photo of your dinner so you could post on social media, or did you take those fifteen minutes to snuggle with your little ones? What's going to mean the most to you when you look back on your life? When you're older, will you compare with others how many Instagram followers you have and how many likes you get? Or will you recall family vacations and good times with your loved ones? We're all given twenty-four hours in the day. How will you spend your time? Scrolling through social media? Social media can be great to connect with others and view positive messages, but it can also lead to negative feelings of comparison. And it can take us away from precious moments with our friends, family, and relationships.

Here's a challenge for you: the next time you're out and about, look around. How many people do you see on their devices, totally ignoring the friends and maybe even the spouse near them? Have you ever found yourself on the social media hamster wheel? You know, when you're just scrolling and scrolling and before you know it, it's been hours? It's so easy to do. But what if we took the time we spent scrolling and spent it with God instead? Or if we spent it with a spouse or our kids or our parents? Wouldn't spending the time with our Creator and our loved ones be more meaningful? Spending time on our devices is definitely popular these days, but is it the healthiest way to spend our days? Ask God how to help you get off the wheel and enjoy the world around you.

YOU GOT THIS!

I challenge you to put down your phone and start living and creating memories outside the screen. Take a walk outside—look at the sunshine, grab a coffee with a friend. Let's reduce the screen time and increase the real face time with others. We don't want to conform to this world but look to the One above.

GOD PROVIDES

Look at the birds of the air: they neither sow nor reap nor gather into barns, and yet your heavenly Father feeds them. Are you not of more value than they? And which of you by being anxious can add a single hour to his span of life? And why are you anxious about clothing? Consider the lilies of the field, how they grow: they neither toil nor spin, yet I tell you, even Solomon in all his glory was not arrayed like one of these. But if God so clothes the grass of the field, which today is alive and tomorrow is thrown into the oven, will he not much more clothe you, O you of little faith? Therefore do not be anxious, saying, "What shall we eat?" or "What shall we drink?" or "What shall we wear?"

MATTHEW 6:26–31 ESV

Did you ever ride a roller coaster as a kid? We'd go to the local amusement park, get in line, and wait for what seemed like forever, and then finally, we'd get to pick our favorite seats on our favorite roller coaster. Buckling in, the alarm sounded, and we were off! Flipping and twisting through the air, we felt light, excited, and happy. Then a few minutes later, the ride was over. All that waiting for a few moments of happiness and then it was done.

A lot of times we want to get to a certain destination. We ask God, "Please help me find my husband" or "Please help me get this job," thinking only that then we'll be happy. But the destination doesn't always equal happiness. Think back to the roller coaster, and enjoy the ride you're on now. Don't think about the next ride you'll go on, but enjoy the flips and turns, the ups and downs where you are now. Enjoy the moment rather than wishing it away. Looking back on your younger years, don't you wish that you hadn't worried about how God would provide for you? Look how far you've come! Have faith!

YOU GOT THIS!

What were times in your life that you wished for what was next? The next time you find yourself hoping for the future and worrying about what's coming, remember where you came from and enjoy where you are. Have faith that God is already taking care of you and knows your next steps. Believe in yourself and in Him!

WORTH ISN'T MEASURED

I can do all things through him who strengthens me.

PHILIPPIANS 4:13 ESV

When we're working, we often have a lot on our plates. We try to get everything done in a hurry, which can leave the work done but not done well. It's when we work smarter rather than harder that we can accomplish more and relieve ourselves of trying to be in the fast lane. Your worth isn't measured by your productivity. This is a huge truth here. Let's read that again: your worth isn't measured by your productivity. Your worth isn't in how clean you can make your house or how happy you can make your boss. It isn't in how many hours you work each day or how well you did the dishes. Your worth is found in Jesus. And guess what—no matter whether you take time to rest or you work until midnight, you are still worthy. God wants you to be happy and not toil with the stresses that come with working hard. It's okay to ask for help. Your worth will not be less. Don't find yourself matching your worth to your paycheck. It's better to make less money and be happier than to work your life away to make money you don't even have time to use. There will always be times when you need to put in the extra effort in your work, whether it is at home or away from home, and that's okay. You're doing what you've been called to do. It's in the busier times that we need to call upon the

Lord for the strength to get through. Work and life get stressful, but we have to remember that we can't work our lives away. If you're working to show your worth, rethink what you're doing each day.

YOU GOT THIS!

What do you enjoy most about what you do every day? Are you measuring your worth by measuring your productivity level? Give yourself grace and allow yourself the freedom to release your worth in Jesus Christ and not in your job or the tasks you accomplish each day. Checking off the to-do list always feels good, but it doesn't compare to the peace we receive when we know that no matter what we get done today, God loves us, He treasures us, and He delights in our existence.

he has madething everyt beautiful in his time

- Ecclesiastes 3:11

YOU CAN
START OVER ANYTIME

Now therefore, if you will indeed obey my voice and keep my covenant, you shall be my treasured possession among all peoples, for all the earth is mine.

EXODUS 19:5 ESV

A lot of times we can feel stuck, as if we have to carry on as we did the day before. We feel stuck in jobs that no longer serve us or stuck in situations that are hurtful to the soul. But the good news is, we can start over anytime, any day, anywhere. When we feel like the walls are closing in on us, that's when we should look for help from above. We aren't planted. We can pull up the roots, no matter how deep, and move to where we can grow better. When the soil is no longer nourishing us and we can't see the sunshine, maybe it's time to make a move—a move that will revive our souls. There's a reason we are where we are, but sometimes we're called to leave that situation, that job, or maybe even friend groups.

Is God nudging you to make a move? If so, don't be scared. God is always with us, even when we can't see it. He's with us through the transition times and gives us everything we need to walk a new path. When jobs or situations no longer serve us, He will provide a way out. It's up to us to accept His invitation and let Him guide the way. It's not always easy, but trusting Him leads to unlocking amazing things we never thought possible.

YOU GOT THIS! *Think about a time in your life when you were feeling unsettled. Maybe you're in that position right now. Maybe you've been there for a while. What are you being drawn toward? What are you being drawn away from? If you're feeling stuck and unsure about changing your path, take it to the Lord. He's already making plans for you. When you begin to listen to His calling you, take action and know you don't have to be afraid to start over again.*

LESS IS MORE

Sell your possessions, and give to the needy. Provide yourselves with moneybags that do not grow old, with a treasure in the heavens that does not fail, where no thief approaches and no moth destroys. For where your treasure is, there will your heart will be also.

LUKE 12:33–34 ESV

We live in a day and age where we're bombarded with advertisements to want "more"—the bigger house, the supersized meal, that have-to-have-it infomercial item. . . . The world is pushing things on us even when we're not aware of it. But "more" isn't always better. We can start to envy those who have "more" than we do. And it's so easy to believe that our value is measured by how many things we have. Yet when we start putting our heart and worth in the amount we have or don't have, it's even easier to lose sight of the treasures above. If we allow ourselves to believe the world's lie, we will never have the peace or contentment that comes with understanding how valuable we are in God's eyes.

What would happen if we stopped storing our value in what's on earth and traded it for our treasures in heaven? What would it look like if, instead of wanting more and more things, we wanted to give more and more away to those in need? Ask yourself, are you giving in the hopes of getting something in return? Or are you giving with a grateful heart, knowing you're helping someone who truly needs what you have to give? Whether it is as small as a loaf of bread or as large as a new bedroom suite, there is always someone who not only has needs but would be genuinely thankful for your servitude.

Maybe it's time to check your heart. Matthew 6:1–4 says, "Beware of practicing your righteousness before other people in order to be seen by them, for then you will have no reward from your Father who is in heaven. Thus, when you give to the needy, sound no trumpet before you, as the hypocrites do in the synagogues and in the streets, that they may be praised by others. Truly, I say to you, they have received their reward. But when you give to the needy, do not let your left hand know what your right hand is doing, so that your giving may be in secret. And your Father who sees in secret will reward you" (ESV).

YOU GOT THIS!

Is it time for a reality check? What are you wanting more of? Instead of filling your home with bins of old clothes, unused playpens, and never-to-be-used-again keepsakes, I challenge you to go through what you have and give things away that no longer serve you, with wanting nothing in return. When you give to others in need, you'll be a blessing to them. Remember, God loves a cheerful giver. So sing and rejoice as you pack up and deliver your donations. Think about how your unused items will bless their next owners and smile.

WORKING SMARTER
VERSUS HARDER

Whatever you do, work heartily,
as for the Lord and not for men.

COLOSSIANS 3:23 ESV

We've all experienced days when it seems as if our work is never done. Even when we cross off the to-do list for the day, we still have yard work, laundry, grocery shopping, a report that needs to be run, another work "fire drill" that pops up in the middle of the day . . . it can easily leave us feeling anxious and defeated. Maybe it's time to examine how we complete our work, both in and outside of the home. Think about it: Is there a repetitive task you are doing that is taking a while to complete? Could it be time to start working smarter instead of harder? We can work hard on a task, but finding a more efficient way to complete it (or finding someone who is better at completing it) can help ease the anxiety and help us work smarter.

Is there a task you are facing right now that seems like a mountain to climb? Have you thought about asking for help? There's no shame in reaching out to a neighbor or a coworker who excels at the very task that is intimidating to you. A lot of times we don't feel comfortable asking for help, fearing that it shows weakness. We feel we should be able to power through and do it all on our own. We hold burdens and cause ourselves stress, when the truth is, if we would just put out a branch, we'd realize that there are others who would love to help us.

When the days and hours seem long, we have to remember what we learned in Colossians 3:23. We're not working for us or for other men but for the Lord. God reminds us throughout Scripture to work hard and not to slack off. So when things get tough, don't hesitate to look for ways to be more efficient, and ask others to help so that you can continue working well and working for the Lord.

YOU GOT THIS! *Think of a few areas where you could use some help. Do you know anyone who loves doing those things? In which areas do you have talent? How can you help others who may need assistance? Think outside the box—outside of work or the home. When we help others and receive help ourselves, we can lessen our stress and feel good about helping those in need.*

CHASING SLOW

And he said, "My presence will go with you,
and I will give you rest."

EXODUS 33:14 ESV

Don't you just love vacation? There's just something about getting away, even if it's for the day. We leave work and life behind to go and enjoy. The world wants us to speed up— we work fast, drive fast, cook fast, clean fast, look fast . . . and we find that when we slow down and enjoy life, we're more at peace. But what if we lived more like that each day? What if we decided to deliberately chase slow rather than fast? What if we actually took that hour lunch break or took the time to sit outside and watch the stars? What if we didn't strive to work so much or pursue the paycheck? What if we chose a career that fulfilled us but didn't drain us? When we live in the fast lane, we can easily get burned out . . . and we were designed with the need to recharge.

We often want what's next in life, and we keep going as fast as we can until we get there. But then what? Well, we chase the next thing . . . but when does it stop? Maybe today you'll give yourself permission to dismiss your to-do list and instead do something that brings you joy. Start making time for what you cherish in life, while accomplishing your God-given purpose. God reminds us in Genesis 2:2–3: "And on the seventh day God finished his work that he had done, and he rested on the seventh day from all his work that he had done. So God blessed the seventh day and made it holy, because on it God rested from all his work that he had done in creation" (ESV). Even God took time to rest, and He wants us to know that it is okay to take time away (and not just on vacation days but every day) from our full, task-filled lives.

YOU GOT THIS!

When you think of the word slow, what comes to mind? Maybe sitting on a front porch in the South, sipping on sweet tea, and watching the sunset . . . or maybe it's sitting on a beach, toes in the sand, while the warm sun rests upon your face. Take what slow looks like to you and start making changes in your life toward it. When you slow things down and don't put so much pressure on yourself, you'll find more peace . . . and that's what God longs for us to have—His peace in and outside ourselves.

PULLING THE WEEDS

Know this, my beloved brothers: let every person be quick to hear, slow to speak, slow to anger; for the anger of man does not produce the righteousness of God. Therefore put away all filthiness and rampant wickedness and receive with meekness the implanted word, which is able to save your souls.

JAMES 1:19–21 ESV

Each day, new problems and challenges arise. Often we push them to the side and deal with them later. Did you ever leave the dishes in the sink after dinner and wait until the next morning to wash them? That baked chicken is definitely not coming off now without soaking the pan. Or what about weeds growing in your yard? The longer you let them grow, the more they spread, the deeper the roots get, and the harder they are to pull out when you tackle the job. We tend to let our problems grow like this. Is something currently bothering you—a situation that you just can't seem to get out of your head? While some circumstances are hard to face head-on—trust me, I know—they may be even harder to deal with when they start to grow roots and spread. It could be time to "nip it in the bud," as they say. This can apply to your job too—it's best to put out that fire you came upon before it spreads.

Sometimes we want to sweep our problems under the proverbial rug or leave them buried, but this is when they can really take hold of our heart. Sometimes we hide our pain for years and are surprised when it pops up out of nowhere and hurts us again. It's only when we bring our problems and pains into the light that we can find true restoration and relief. While it's true that God heals all wounds in time, the wounds aren't fully cleaned to heal properly if they aren't addressed. Perhaps it's time to work with Him to deal with the ones coming to mind today.

YOU GOT THIS!

Can you recall a time or situation where you have buried past pains or problems? What are you pushing aside today? A relationship that needs healing or something that needs to be addressed at home? Don't wait. Even if you want to sweep it under the rug and deal with it later, you'll feel much better once everything is done and sorted out.

SAYING NO

Let what you say be simply 'Yes' or 'No'; anything more than this comes from evil.

MATTHEW 5:37 ESV

How do you feel about the word no? It generally gives a negative feeling. As women we take on everything, and it can leave us both satisfied and burned out. We agree to do things that we'd rather not just to please others and make them happy. We often say yes to things we don't even have time for, and why? Because we don't want to hurt anyone's feelings. What if we started to look at the word no in a positive way? And what if we started living in the yes by saying yes to ourselves and our health and no to what depletes us? After all, the no to something leaves an open opportunity for someone else to take that on as a yes. Saying no to a new job that isn't quite what we wanted leaves a yes for someone who's always dreamed of obtaining that role. Saying no to going on another date when we don't think he's "a good match" leaves a yes for someone else to find their soulmate. When we stop thinking of no as a bad word, we can start living in a yes world—a world that allows us the freedom to do what's best for us and what God created us to do.

A no to something could be the perfect yes to what God is calling us to. When it comes to work, we do sometimes have to say yes and roll up our sleeves to get the work done. But when it comes to things that don't feel right down in our soul, it's okay to say no. Maybe no one has ever told you that, or maybe you're so used to making sure that others are happy that you forgot about making yourself happy. I'm here to remind you that it's okay to think of yourself too!

YOU GOT THIS! *What are you saying yes to that you know deserves a true no? How can you see the word no in a positive light? Have you ever been told no before and took it the hard way? The next time someone says no, rethink how you take their answer. When we start believing that no isn't so bad, we can start listening to the calling of our heart and follow God's lead!*

ADDING MORE
TO OUR PLATE

Cast all your anxiety on Him because He cares for you.

I PETER 5:7 NIV

Have you ever had too much to eat for dinner? Picture yourself in a fancy restaurant: you just finished a three-course meal, and you're stuffed. The waiter comes around with the dessert cart and everything looks fantastic. You say, "I'll have dessert!" It tastes so good at the time, but soon after, stomach pains set in and you wonder why in the world you splurged on the sweet treat. "Was it worth it?" you ask yourself.

If we're not careful, we can fill up our lives in the same way. When we have so much to do and put too much on our proverbial plates, our body, soul, and mind hurt. Instead of enjoying the meal and feeling good, we feel the pain. When we constantly do this to ourselves, we don't allow ourselves to enjoy life. And isn't life meant to be lived? Weren't we designed to fill up on its goodness instead of feeling as if we are left empty? Here's a new concept: you can have a full life without having to fill it to the brim each day. We often try to get as much done as we can, and while it can be fulfilling to cross items off our lists, days and days of this toil can leave us feeling deeply unsatisfied. As women, we are good at taking on more than we can do, and as mothers, wives, daughters, sisters, coworkers, and more, we juggle so much. It's okay not to sign up for that PTA meeting or take on that bake sale or coaching the upcoming soccer game. When it starts to as if you're running on empty, maybe it's time to consider asking for help. Think of someone you can trust—someone at work and at home—who could take off some of the pressure. You might even want to start looking for more efficient ways to tackle your tasks and make decisions.

And don't forget to pray. Ask God for help! God tends to send help in many different ways, so be on the lookout. Just watch—He'll show up for you, providing ways for you to find help and rest. All you have to do is lay it at His feet.

YOU GOT THIS!

How are you feeling with all you have going on each day? What's something on your plate that you should reduce or eliminate? There are seasons of life when we do carry a lot, but seek out what you enjoy and see what you can take off your plate or what can be done differently to bring more time to your day. Often we feel uneasy in asking for help, but when we do, new doors will be opened.

REGROUP

It is in vain that you rise up early and go late to rest, eating the bread of anxious toil; for he gives to his beloved sleep.

PSALM 127:2 ESV

When I was young, my aunt would always say, "Okay, let's regroup" after we would come home after one of our girls' trips. I knew that she meant it was time to recalibrate—time to breathe, unwind, and rest. But it wasn't until I was older that I appreciated what it meant to "regroup." After a long, hard day, sometimes we just want to go home and "regroup." Too often we are like the Energizer Bunny—we want to keep going and going, without stopping to appreciate the small things. And it's hard to get off the hamster wheel long enough to look around us and enjoy God's beautiful creation.

For many of us, the need to stay busy isn't our fault. We learned in grade school to stay busy. It started during school hours, but many of us also went to after-school activities—soccer, dance, swim team—and then we went home to piles of homework, and we studied for tests until bedtime. We were never advised to just stop and be a kid and relax. So we continued to run on the hamster wheel throughout high school, and it has continued into adulthood. Think about it. Even when we get rare weekends free, aren't they jam-packed with activities or cleaning the house? Maybe it's time to regroup—to recharge our batteries. Even our phones need recharging. Do you give yourself time to rest and recharge, or do you go until you burn out?

YOU GOT THIS!

So many of us are used to going and going and going, and this leads to burnout. We need to give ourselves time to enjoy life. Even watching the ocean or a campfire can be soothing to the soul. What do you enjoy doing? What recharges your soul? See where in your life you can start making changes so that you give yourself time to rest and regroup.

HOW DO YOU
SEE YOURSELF?

Finally, brothers, whatever is true, whatever is honorable, whatever is just, whatever is pure, whatever is lovely, whatever is commendable, if there is any excellence, if there is anything worthy of praise, think about these things.

PHILIPPIANS 4:8 ESV

Sometimes we can be the hardest on ourselves. When we don't get everything done that we wanted to . . . when we're late for an important meeting . . . when we can't find the important thing we're supposed to do something with. . . .Before you know it, the negative self-talk starts spinning out of control. We tell ourselves we're failing at life, we can't accomplish the task in front of us, we're not pretty enough, we're not good enough, and everyone on earth knows we're worthless—and there couldn't be anything further from the truth. Maybe it's time to start building ourselves up so we don't fall for the lies.

How do we do this? Enter: Jesus. He sees beyond any faults you see in yourself. He wants you to give yourself grace, the same grace He gives you! When we know our worth and whose we are, we can stand firm and stand against the negative self-talk. When you start to believe the lies, remember, God says that you are beautiful—inside and out. He says you are one-of-a-kind, He treasures you, He values you, and He created you in His image. When we remember those truths, we can choose to live in the light of Jesus. Each moment of the day we choose how we react to situations. We can't choose what happens to us or what people think of us, but we can choose how we react to those things. The next time you hear yourself going down a path of negative self-talk, ask God to take those thoughts out of your head and then watch as He shines light in the darkness and changes your frown into a smile!

YOU GOT THIS!

The next time you're faced with negative self-talk, ask God to turn it around. Remind yourself of who God says you are. And instead of getting angry or sad, let His light shine through. The best thing we can put on in the morning is a smile. When we are thankful and grateful, we can start to see the beauty in our lives rather than focusing on what all went wrong. Today, I challenge you to live in the present moment instead of the past. Speak only positive self-talk, and think only of the beautiful gifts God gave you!

JESUS HAS OVERCOME

I have said these things to you, that in me you may have peace. In the world you will have tribulation. But take heart; I have overcome the world.

JOHN 16:33 ESV

Have you ever had one of those days when the world seemed to be crashing down on you? Maybe you got up too late, had a flat tire, spilled your coffee, or missed the bus. We often tend to focus on what's caused us trouble instead of finding the good in it. Maybe you unknowingly got up late so you wouldn't leave at a certain time, avoiding an accident. Or maybe you accidentally spilled your coffee so you'd end up waiting a few minutes, in order to pass by an old friend on your way to work.

What would happen if we started to view our obstacles as opportunities? What if we tried to view the hurdles through the eyes of God? After all, He sees what we cannot and knows what we need more than we do. God is working out all things for the good of His children, which means it's not just our story that we are living for. We're all connected. Our actions affect others and vice versa. We have to remember that through it all, God is holding the universe together, and we need not worry or ask why. We just need to live in His peace and trust. The good news is, we already know that the battle has been won! Good wins over evil. God wants us to live in a posture of peace over worry and tribulation. When things aren't going as we planned, let's remember that they're going as He planned.

YOU GOT THIS!

The next time an obstacle comes your way, practice not fretting about it. Instead, remember that God's got this! It may be hard to realize in the moment, but try not to let yourself get anxious or upset about it. Instead, learn to live in a presence of grace. When you lean on God and know that He has your best interests in mind, you'll be able to ease through times like these.

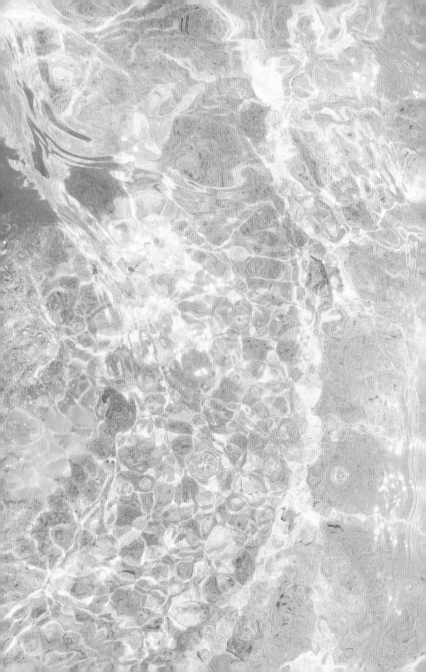

She was beautiful, but not like those girls in the magazines. She was beautiful for the way she thought. She was beautiful for the sparkle in her eyes when she talked about something she loved. She was beautiful for her ability to make other people smile, even if she was sad. No, she wasn't beautiful for something as temporary as her looks. She was beautiful, deep down to her soul.

- F. SCOTT FITZGERALD

GOOD SHEPHERD

My sheep hear my voice,
and I know them, and they follow me.

JOHN 10:27 ESV

Maybe you've heard before that Jesus is the Good Shepherd. Ever wonder what that means? Jesus explains in John 10:7–16: "So Jesus again said to them, 'Truly, truly, I say to you, I am the door of the sheep. All who came before me are thieves and robbers, but the sheep did not listen to them. I am the door. If anyone enters by me, he will be saved and will go in and out and find pasture. The thief comes only to steal and kill and destroy. I came that they may have life and have it abundantly. I am the good shepherd. The good shepherd lays down his life for the sheep . . . I know my own and my own know me, just as the Father knows me and I know the Father; and I lay down my life for the sheep. And I have other sheep that are not of this fold. I must bring them also, and they will listen to my voice. So there will be one flock, one shepherd'" (ESV).

We are the sheep, and Jesus is the Shepherd. He watches over us and sits at the door, making sure that we're safe. Have you had a hard time hearing from God lately? Sometimes it seems that God goes silent on us and we're left wandering around like lost sheep. But maybe, just maybe, He is waiting for us to really listen—to sit by His side all hours of every day and practice listening and tuning into His voice. As a wandering sheep, we need the Shepherd. He guards the door and keeps us safe. When He calls us, we listen and follow Him. We need to know His voice. Know that whether or not you are hearing from Him, the Good Shepherd is always there, tenderly caring for you and longing for you to wholeheartedly lean into Him for all your wants, needs, hopes, and dreams.

YOU GOT THIS!

After glimpsing this picture of Jesus, do you see yourself in the pasture with the other sheep, or are you a wanderer? When the Good Shepherd speaks, can you hear Him? When you learn His voice and listen for when He calls you, follow Him and let Him lead you to what's next!

COMMUNITY VERSUS COMPETITION

Two are better than one, because they have a good reward for their toil. For if they fall, one will lift up his fellow. But woe to him who is alone when he falls and has not another to lift him up! Again, if two lie together, they keep warm, but how can one keep warm alone? And though a man might prevail against one who is alone, two will withstand him—a threefold cord is not quickly broken.

ECCLESIASTES 4:9–12 ESV

What do you think of when you hear the word *competition*? Two well-known rivals that comes to mind are the two most famous fast-food restaurants—McDonald's versus Burger King. Or maybe you thought of your two neighbors fighting over whose lawn looks better. Maybe the word *competition* makes you think about a few small businesses who share the same clients. However you view it, we all know that competition does exist in this life. But what we may not have uncovered yet is the ability to use competition to empower one another.

What if we lifted each other up instead of silently tearing each other down? Think about the industry you're in. How can we push that industry forward rather than push down the individual companies within that industry? Competition can be either healthy or destructive. Healthy competition can push people and businesses to do better and innovate, or competition can be hurtful and frustrating. When everyone plays together nicely in the sandbox and we work toward a common goal, we can help each other grow. We have to remember that someone else's success isn't our failure. Maybe there's someone in the community or industry who needs some help with a task you're really good at. What if you helped lift them up so they can succeed too? What if we joined groups that share common interests and do the same things we do each day, so we could share tips and tricks to help us better ourselves while also bettering the community? What if competition wasn't viewed as a bad thing but rather a way to come together?

YOU GOT THIS!

Take a look at your industry, your competition, and your community. Where can you use your gifts and talents for the greater good? It only takes one person to start making good changes. How can you make an impact and a difference in your circles? When we come together as a community, we can build each other up and bring more positivity to the world.

PRESENT OVER PERFECT

Not that I have already obtained this or am already perfect, but I press on to make it my own, because Christ Jesus has made me his own. Brothers, I do not consider that I have made it my own. But one thing I do: forgetting what lies behind and straining forward to what lies ahead, I press on toward the goal for the prize of the upward call of God in Christ Jesus. Let those of us who are mature think this way, and if in anything you think otherwise, God will reveal that also to you.

PHILIPPIANS 3:12–15 ESV

A lot of us give 110 percent every single day. We just want to do everything correctly, with no flaws, errors, or mistakes. And many days can go by with us actually believing that we are getting everything done with impeccable precision and excellence . . . but the truth is, perfection just isn't attainable for humans. There's no doubt; we will falter. And the sad part is that when we do, the perfectionist inside just can't handle it. Before you know it, we are feeling like unworthy failures, letting negative self-talk run rampant in our minds.

During these times, let's try to remember that there has only been one perfect being to have ever walked the earth, and His name is Jesus. No life is perfect and no situation is perfect, even if they seem to be that way on the outside. We can't get everything done that we want to do and also have time for a million other things. Sometimes we can feel like we've failed when we don't get to accomplish or experience certain things. What if, instead of striving for perfection, we just do the best we can in each moment? What if we strive to be present in life instead of always doing 110 percent? What if we took a moment to call a friend or kissed our kids instead of running out to do x, y, and z? What if we learn to soak in the day we're given? What if we were fully present while out with our friends and family rather than wondering what's waiting for us back at work? Even though it may be hard, try to remove yourself from work when you're away from work. We all need balance in life, and when our minds are constantly consumed with things concerning work, we cannot fully be present where we are. Give yourself grace today. Practice faithfulness over flawlessness. We learn from the Scriptures to forget what happened before and look forward to what lies ahead.

YOU GOT THIS! *How can you start practicing to be present in your life instead of striving for perfection, which is a hill we cannot climb? When we realize that we are imperfect beings, we can rest assured that there is a perfect Someone who is making our paths straight. When we start living in the present, our anxieties can be cast away, knowing God has us in His hands.*

FIGHTING
YOUR BATTLES

And whatever you do, in word or deed,
do everything in the name of the Lord Jesus,
giving thanks to God the Father through him.

COLOSSIANS 3:17 ESV

Life is busy. And when we're running from one place to another, it's really easy to forget why we're doing what we're doing. We can chase success, recognition, status . . . which can all lead to stress. What we need is a daily check-in with our hearts. What do you love about what you do each day? It's when we lose ourselves in work and forget the why that our jobs and lives becomes stressful. Sometimes we need this reality check to keep moving forward. If a job is no longer serving you, take a look to examine where your heart is and pray. If we all do what we enjoy and are best at, the world will be a better place. We spend a lot of our lives working, so shouldn't we enjoy it?

Do you feel as if you're in the wrong position in life? As if you are out of place? Think about it and take money out of the equation. What would you enjoy doing each day? Now what's stopping you from doing that? If God has given you the gifts and is moving your heart in that direction, He will provide. Maybe there's something out there that you will love and have not even explored yet. Or maybe you're satisfied with where you are and excited for the growth opportunities to come. We can work as hard as we're able, but we have to make sure we're doing it for the glory of God, using the talents and gifts He's given and in the position He desires us to be in.

YOU GOT THIS!

As you think about your career or your daily work, give thanks to the Lord for what He's given you—good and bad. They've all brought you where you are today and will pave the way for your future. Check in with your heart on your level of happiness. What gifts do you possess? What do you do best at? People change jobs all the time, but it's when we get in the position where we feel comfortable and "needed" that the desires of our hearts and souls are met and we can finally feel at peace.

WHAT OTHERS THINK

The fear of man lays a snare,
but whoever trusts in the LORD is safe.

PROVERBS 29:25 ESV

Do you ever worry about what others think of you? Maybe you received a bad evaluation at work, or maybe your company received a bad customer review online. It could be that you're too afraid to ask that guy out on a date because you're worried what your friends will think of you. Those kinds of situations make us believe that we're failures or aren't good enough. What others think about us—whether they said it about us or we believe they think it about us—can cause anxiety. When we place more worth and weight on the way others feel about us than we place on how God feels about us, it may be time for a self-check. One thing to always keep in mind: the world isn't out to get you. While we have a real enemy who wants us to sink deep into our insecurities, these false truths or lies can eat away at our soul. People don't spend their days thinking bad things about you. How often do you spend your time thinking poorly of others? Not a lot, right?

On top of the fact that people aren't spending their days thinking about how bad you are, why would you care if they were? It's your life, not theirs. Why do you put worth in what others think and say when your worth is already found in Jesus? When we are constantly worried about what others think of us, it's possible we'll miss out on many awesome opportunities that God has planned. Our Redeemer loves and cares for you; He would never put you down or call you unworthy. He longs to set you free from the prison of untrue thoughts and feelings. So the next time you start worrying about what others think of you, why not ask God to erase those thoughts from your mind and fill your heart with His love instead?

YOU GOT THIS!

We can be our biggest critics. Instead, be your biggest cheerleader! Surround yourself with positivity, and when the negativity comes in, push it out. Focus your eyes on Jesus and pray. Do good things for others and fill your soul with the good. Tell yourself good things about yourself. Remember, those who mind don't matter, and those who matter don't mind. When you feel the negativity creeping in, know that you are capable and worthy! You are a daughter of the King! Jesus loves you. He always has and always will.

WORK HARD
AND STAY HUMBLE

*Beware of practicing your righteousness before other people
in order to be seen by them, for then you will have no reward
from your Father who is in heaven. Thus, when you give to
the needy, sound no trumpet before you, as the hypocrites do
in the synagogues and in the streets, that they may be praised
by others. Truly, I say to you, they have received their reward.
But when you give to the needy, do not let your left hand know
what your right hand is doing, so that your giving may be in
secret. And your Father who sees in secret will reward you.*

MATTHEW 6:1–4 ESV

Did you come from a hardworking family, or did you become a
hard worker on your own? Either way, this devotional is meant
for you. You work hard each day, doing what you're called
to do, in this moment, in this time, right where you're at in
life. Maybe you're a stay-at-home mom or a girl just finishing
college . . . or an executive or a working mom or a combination!

As women we have a lot going on, inside and outside of
the home. We have small and big wins, and God wants us to
celebrate each and every one of them! Maybe your son is finally
eating carrots, or you're getting the next position up. No matter

the win, God is cheering you on. Your win is also God's win.

Sometimes the wins keep coming! If that describes your current season of life, celebrate your Father, the One who got you where you are today. Celebrate the fact that the Creator of the universe is working through you for His glory. That's a big statement to remember! We're all working for His kingdom, not our own. We're His daughters. The wins are to be celebrated, that's for sure! It's when we remember who got us there that we can humble ourselves and keep pushing forward, with His help and guidance.

YOU GOT THIS!

The next time you have a win (whether big or small), take a little time to celebrate with God and thank Him for the gifts He graciously gave you. Keep on working hard—for His glory, not your own. Keep a note not to brag about what you have done, not to give yourself all the credit, and let God's light shine through you!

USING THE
BEST CHINA

And this is the confidence that we have toward him, that
if we ask anything according to his will he hears us. And
if we know that he hears us in whatever we ask, we know
that we have the requests that we have asked of him.

I JOHN 5:14–15 ESV

Do you remember going to a relative's house for gatherings while growing up? Maybe your grandma brought out her best china for Christmas dinner. Then it was washed and put away, waiting for the next holiday. Or maybe you've gotten a beautiful gift that was too nice to wear or use, so you tucked it away. Why do we only use our "best" things when it's a special occasion and tuck them away because they're "too good for everyday use"? Maybe you feel that way about talking to God. Maybe you only go to Him when it's a big emergency. We learn in Luke 11:9–10, "And I tell you, ask, and it will be given to you; seek, and you will find; knock, and it will be opened to you. For everyone who asks receives, and the one who seeks finds, and to the one who knocks it will be opened" (ESV). God is the good china, but He is always accessible! In fact, He wants us to have deep roots—to know Him and to lean on Him, so that when the storms come, He grounds us in His Word. Don't feel as if He has to be tucked away and only called on every so often. We're reminded in I Thessalonians 5:16–18, "Rejoice always, pray without ceasing, give thanks in all circumstances; for this is the will of God in Christ Jesus for you" (ESV).

YOU GOT THIS!

Do you have something you've put away for a special occasion? The next time you break it out, think about this: you can always come and talk to God—anytime, anywhere, and about anything. He is always listening. When we start having a relationship with God and remember that He is accessible outside trying times, our roots will start to grow as we grow in our relationship with the One Most High.

ALLOWED TO BE HAPPY!

I have said these things to you,
that in me you may have peace. In the world you will have
tribulation. But take heart; I have overcome the world.

JOHN 16:33 ESV

Peace . . . there's just something softening about that word. It means no tribulation, no fighting, no sadness—just a softened, pure, at-ease state. God reminds us in the Book of John that we aren't promised a perfect life. The world will have tribulation, of that there's no doubt. It always has, it always will. Not all our days will be easy. We may spill our coffee over us right as we walk through the door . . . the kids can be screaming and not listening . . . we could have failed the test that we really needed to pass . . . we could miss out on an opportunity . . . we could have not gotten the job we desired. The list could go on. Disappointments are a part of life, but that doesn't mean we have to live in the shadows. In fact, we are called to do the complete opposite. We are called to step out into the light of Christ.

When we're down, sometimes we find it easier to just stay there, to bask in our sorrows and look for everything that's bad in life and hang on to them. And in some cases, we can become scared to actually be happy because we are always waiting for the other shoe to drop. Instead of letting God's peace and joy fill our heart, we worry about what bad thing is going to happen next. Want some fabulous news? God has overcome the world. He has overcome sadness and darkness. He wants us to have peace. Let me repeat that—He wants us to have peace. He wants us to be happy and cast all of our fears and anxieties on Him.

Sometimes we put all our hopes into one proverbial basket—if I get this job or if I get this promotion or if I get everything on my task list done today, then I'll be happy. But just because we badly want something to happen, it doesn't mean that it's meant for us, and we have to be okay with the fact that God knows much more than we can ever imagine. We're reminded of this in Romans 8:28: "And we know that for those who love God all things work together for good, for those who are called according to his purpose" (ESV). God has overcome the world, and He will overcome anything you're going through.

YOU GOT THIS!

What are you upset about right now? What's keeping you from being truly happy? Take an inventory of your heart and soul. What can you give to God today so you can be at peace? The past is the past and God wants you to look forward, to the light of Jesus, not stay in the shadows. When you feel as if you can't be happy, be reminded that there's nothing God can't overcome.

TRUSTING GOD

The LORD is my strength and my shield;
in him my heart trusts, and I am helped; my heart exults,
and with my song I give thanks to him.

PSALM 28:7 ESV

Have you ever had a hard time trusting others to "take the wheel"? You know, like that unsettled feeling you get after sending your husband to the grocery store or the uneasiness that hits you after agreeing to let your brother pick out the gift for your mom this year.

As women, we try to do it all, even when it comes to planning our lives. But attempting to do it all, all the time, can be overwhelming and ultimately lead us to wanting to give up. So what do you say we try something else? What if we tried to just give "the wheel" to Jesus? That's a big move, right? Giving up control can be tough. But, honestly, can't we trust that God has it all figured out for us already?

Think about the last time you were on an airplane. Now, this may scare some people, but what if the pilot walked over to you and said, "Here, [your name], your turn! I'm going to sit back, relax, and enjoy the flight"? I'm sure you would be like, "Wait, what? I can't do this! I'm not a pilot!" (Or maybe you are, so hang tight for this exercise!) God's job is not your job.

You weren't meant to take over and fly the plane or steer the car of your life. That's what God's supposed to do. But you can't just "sit back and enjoy the ride" either. God won't drop off everything He wants for you on your doorstep like an Amazon package. However, He is in charge, and those twists and turns in life will have you meet the people you need to have in your life during certain times, and He will give you the nudges to do certain things. When things don't go as planned, that's just not what God intended for you. Sometimes pilots have to navigate around storms, and other times they have to go right through them. Either way, life is so much easier when we lean into God as our guide and stay attuned to the awesome plans He has in store for us.

YOU GOT THIS!

Is it scary to give up control? God won't just hand us everything we're working toward. We have to work for it. We will have highs and lows and twists and turns. Really, no path is ever straight and easy. The next time you want to be in control, remember who has the reins and who has you in the palm of His hand.

RESTORATION

Heal me, LORD, and I will be healed;
save me and I will be saved, for You are the One I praise.

JEREMIAH 17:14 NIV

Do you like watching those DIY, fixer-upper shows? Design and contractor teams can see what's possible even when bright orange paint and dirty carpets are everywhere. They look at a space and know what walls should be knocked down. They can see beyond the mess.

Think about this—God sees you and your situations the same way. When we see the messiness inside or the walls we've built up in our heart and mind, God sees a beautiful house just waiting to be restored. Are you in a season of needing a renovation? He can knock down the walls, sweep up the dirt, add a little paint, and have your soul feeling new, fresh, and ready to shine!

We all have stuff buried deep inside our soul that we'd rather not deal with, and sometime our restoration process can get pretty messy and dusty. But isn't it worth working through it with God to get on the other side of things with a clean slate? When we clean up the mess in our lives and work through our problems with God, we'll start living in a cleaner, freer, more peaceful space. It's when things are dirty and we don't want to face them (or we're terrified to acknowledge them) that we keep on feeling it's okay to live this way. He sees your mess, and He's not afraid of it. He also sees your potential. He loves you. Now it's time to do the walk-through and see how to make your house shine.

YOU GOT THIS!

Have you ever seen yourself as a house needing to be fixed up? In which areas of your life (or rooms) do you need to do the most cleaning or reorganizing? Which needs to have just a touch of paint? Maybe the whole house needs to be gutted and remade into something beautiful. Take a look at where you can use some updates in your soul and mind; it may get dusty and dirty, but it'll be a cleaner "house" to live in.

His plans for me are good

-jeremiah 29:11

YOUR GARDEN

Hear then the parable of the sower: When anyone hears the word of the kingdom and does not understand it, the evil one comes and snatches away what has been sown in his heart. This is what was sown along the path. As for what was sown on rocky ground, this is the one who hears the word and immediately receives it with joy, yet he has no root in himself, but endures for a while, and when tribulation or persecution arises on account of the word, immediately he falls away. As for what was sown among thorns, this is the one who hears the word, but the cares of the world and the deceitfulness of riches choke the word, and it proves unfruitful. As for what was sown on good soil, this is the one who hears the word and understands it. He indeed bears fruit and yields, in one case a hundredfold, in another sixty, and in another thirty.

MATTHEW 13:18–23 ESV

Have you ever planted a garden? If so, you know it takes seeds to produce fruit and vegetables. Drying, freezing, and lots of good water help the seeds produce good crops. When we don't give the plants enough water—or when we give them too much water—they can fade away. We can plant the seeds, but if we don't tend to them properly and give them good, nourishing soil, they can't grow and no fruit will come from them. I love today's Scripture in Matthew because it paints such a great picture of how we can learn to root ourselves in God. The Word is the seed, and when we read His Word, listen to His voice, and obey His commands, our roots get stronger. Then, when the storms of life come, we're able to withstand the winds because we have the deep roots—we have grounded ourselves in God's everlasting peace and sustaining hope.

You see, while seeds need good soil in order to take root, grow, and bear fruit, the soul needs to be rooted in God's Word to become stronger in its faith. When we start living with Him and for Him, our seeds begins to bear fruit not only for ourselves but also for the lives around us. When we understand and strengthen our faith, it's then that we can truly help friends, family members, passersby, and all who happen to cross our path. We may even be able to help them strengthen their own roots in the Spirit.

YOU GOT THIS!

How can you best tend to your "garden"? Are you planting the right seeds and also giving the seeds enough nourishment? If the seed was scattered in your garden, what would your soil look like? Are there any thorns lingering—or rocky soil? When we can provide a nourishing and fruitful spot for the seeds sown in us, deep roots will form that can't be easily shaken.

THE TOUGH BOSS

Be still before the LORD and wait patiently for him; fret not yourself over the one who prospers in his way, over the man who carries out evil devices! Refrain from anger, and forsake wrath! Fret not yourself; it tends only to evil. For the evildoers shall be cut off, but those who wait for the LORD shall inherit the land.

PSALM 37:7–9 ESV

We've all been there, one time or another. . . . I'm talking about getting a tough boss. Sometimes, no matter what we do, it is never good enough. This can leave us feeling unworthy, challenging our job choice, our company, and even our career. Maybe the boss never gives necessary days off or they discredit what we've done. Nevertheless, we work for most of our lives, and getting up each day for someone who doesn't make us feel worthy can leave us feeling worthless. The good news is, we're there for a reason. But that can be a hard pill to swallow. God wants us where we are in that moment, to learn and soak up all we can, while He's preparing what's next for us, no matter where that is. We have to remember, the boss is also there for a reason and for a season. God has them in that position.

Bringing one's concerns to the table and having a candid conversation may be successful but still leave us still feeling unsettled or unheard. If this sounds familiar, I would encourage you to take things to God. He's the waymaker. He may open a way for you to move and it will be up to you to take action, even if it's a huge change or makes you feel totally uncomfortable. Remember, though, He's there through it all. Sometimes He's placed us in our current roles because He's working on opening new doors for us. However, if we don't walk through the door He's opened, someone else will still be waiting for that exact position. Now that's what I call full circle.

It may be worth reading that part again: sometimes we are in our current roles because He's working on opening a new one for us, and if we don't leave the one we're in, it won't open the door for someone else who is looking and waiting for that exact position. If you're in this situation now, hold strong and pray. You've got this because He is with you.

YOU GOT THIS!

Having a not-so-nice boss can be rough. Have you been in this situation before—or are you currently in it? When we realize that we are where we are for a reason, it helps us to know that God's already got a plan for us throughout the situation. Sometimes He wants us to stay put, and other times He wants us to make a move.. Take some time today to pray and lean into God. Ask Him to lead and guide you as you think through your next steps.

HOLDING STRONG

So do not fear, for I am with you; do not be dismayed, for I am your God. I will strengthen you and help you; I will uphold you with my righteous right hand.

ISAIAH 41:10 NIV

We all have those days when we just want to give up. We want to give up on everything from our relationships and jobs to our dreams and plans. The world gets to us and people get to us and we're left feeling tired and helpless, in desperate need of a break.

In Isaiah, God says not to be dismayed. He promises to strengthen and help us no matter what we're going through. He is always with us, so we should not have any fear or worry. So, when things get tough and we feel like giving up, it's time to step away and talk to God. Try opening the Bible and seeing what verse pops out. It may be the exact message we need to keep going.

When we spend time with God and His Word, we're strengthening our bond with Him. So when the hard days hit us and we feel like giving up or putting on a movie and crawling into bed, we can lean on God for rest and renewal instead. We can pray and seek Him above any situation. We're in it for a reason and even just for a season. The sun will still come up tomorrow and God provides a fresh start.

YOU GOT THIS!

When you're in a situation where you just want to quit, lean on the One Most High. Let His Word give you strength and encouragement when you need it the most. When you walk with God continuously, you'll remember He's already there when both the good and bad times come. His Word will become something you can look back on in times of need and in times of praise.

HONORING WORK
AND HOME

*Whatever you do, work heartily, as for the Lord and not for men,
knowing that from the Lord you will receive the inheritance as your
reward. You are serving the Lord Christ.*

COLOSSIANS 3:23–24 ESV

There are days when work just seems to pile up. The dishes get left
in the sink for days, there is no more milk in the refrigerator, and
we want five more minutes of sleep. Whether we work in or out of
the house, we've experienced times when what we do each day takes
over—and when this happens, homes, families, and relationships
suffer. And it can leave us feeling as if we're a bad mom, wife, sister,
or daughter. But it's important to remember who we are and not
what we do. Sometimes the dishes have to wait, and sometimes we
can't answer the phone when our friends call, and sometimes we
have to put off that visit to the grocery store. However, it's when we
find ourselves constantly playing catch-up that this can be hurtful
not only to us but to our home as well.

If we have little ones, we can start getting "mom guilt" and
wondering if what we're doing is right for our kids or our family.
We can be at home with our kids each day and feel the guilt of
not working hard enough. Even if we don't have little ones, we can

feel the guilt working and how it affects our relationships. What God wants us to remember is that everything we do, whether at home or at work, we get to do those tasks not for ourselves but for God and His Kingdom. In fact, He is continuing to work through you even during the most mundane tasks. When you are washing the dishes, He sees you taking care of your family. When you are turning in a report, He sees you delivering excellent work that will ultimately change the direction of your company in a positive way. No matter what we are doing, if we lean into Him, letting Him guide us and shape us as we go about our days, we shouldn't feel guilty or discouraged about what we do each day but rather see our work as a blessing from above.

YOU GOT THIS!

Have you ever felt guilty for what you do each day? Do you have the mom, daughter, sister, or wife guilt? Rest in God's presence and know that God, too, worked hard—and still works hard each day—so you can too! Remember, He gave you great gifts that you are putting to use each day. When you grow weary, be reminded that you're working for the King! And He is cheering you on!

DOING GOOD

And let us not grow weary of doing good,
for in due season we will reap, if we do not give up.

GALATIANS 6:9 ESV

Have you ever done something and wondered, *What's in it for me?* Maybe you helped someone get groceries or finish a report . . . or you brought your friend flowers for her birthday. Those are all good things. Maybe you work hard each day and wonder when you'll see your reward.

God reminds us in Galatians that our good works are not for nothing—and that we shouldn't give up doing good things just because we don't get an instant reward. When you are about to do a good thing, do a heart check. Ask yourself why are you doing it. Is it for your own glory? Is it to get some sort of thankfulness or reward? What if, instead of looking at what's in it for us, we change it around and think about how it will help or bring happiness to someone else? Do you think Jesus ever looked for a reward for His good acts? What if we take a posture like His and not grow weary of doing things that are good? There is so much negativity in the world—what if we start showing some light and not seeking anything in return?

YOU GOT THIS! *What are some ways that you can use your gifts, talents, and more to do good? It can be as simple as paying for someone in front of you. That simple act can have a rippling effect. Maybe the person you did that for will do something special for someone else. When you start wondering "what's in it" for you, take a step back and remember what you learned from Galatians 6:9 and never stop doing good works.*

PRAYING FOR YOUR WORK

Let the favor of the Lord our God be upon us,
and establish the work of our hands upon us; yes,
establish the work of our hands!

PSALM 90:17 ESV

Do you ever pray about the work you do? We tend to pray for others and what we need help with, but what if we prayed for the work we do? It's not about praying to be the next millionaire on the block but rather about glorifying Him through what we do each day. Instead of letting it weigh on our shoulders, how about reaching out to God to help us get through a tough meeting or to celebrate with us when we make the big sale and to guide our heart, hands, and mind to make just the right moves that will lead us to success. And let's not forget to continue to hear and listen for His calling, if it should ever change for us in what He wants us to do each day. We should be glorifying God in what we are called to do and be an example of a daughter of the King where we work. Oftentimes it's taboo to talk about religion in the workplace, but where you work can be a place where you can reach out a hand to a coworker who may not know Jesus or needs to be given some guidance in their lives. Ask whether you can pray for them. It's in these special opportunities that we bring others to Jesus. Let Him bless what you do each day as you work to glorify Him.

YOU GOT THIS!

When you pray, try praying for your work too. Ask Him to watch over your work and to let it bring Him praise. Be open to new opportunities He places in your path. Let Him establish the work of your hands, for His glory.

FOR THE LOVE
OF MONEY

No one can serve two masters, for either he will hate the one and love the other, or he will be devoted to the one and despise the other. You cannot serve God and money.

MATTHEW 6:24 ESV

Do you live to work or work to live? What is the driving force behind your work? We all need the basic necessities to live—food, clothing, water, shelter . . . but when does what you do each day turn into how much you make from it? God reminds us in Matthew that we cannot serve two masters. You cannot love both God and money. The love of money and power drives people to work extremely hard, be deceitful, and make some wrong turns that leave them spiraling spiritually. God knows we need money to live, as it's not right to steal. But we need to look at what we enjoy doing each day and compare it to what we need to make a living. Do you work tirelessly, to get as much money as possible? Are you working for the money, or are you working for the Lord? Sometimes people will take a good paying job because it "pays well," when their talents and heart could be much more satisfied in a job that pays less but serves them better. I'm sure people who have a love for money are coming to your mind right now . . . but let's put them aside and not judge them. Let's take a hard look at where our heart lies. Are you in it for the money or for His glory? If you do make more than enough, you shouldn't feel ashamed of it. You should think of it as a blessing from God. He just wants to remind us not to love money over Him. There are so many wonderful things you can do when you have money to spare to help others.

YOU GOT THIS!

How did you feel after your heart check? Where does your soul lie? It's never too late to rethink how we think about money. If you have extra resources, is there a business or a charity that can use some extra help? Remember, God loves you, but He does not want you to love money and serve it over Him.

GOD NEVER CHANGES

For I the LORD do not change; therefore you,
O children of Jacob, are not consumed.

MALACHI 3:6 ESV

In an ever-changing world, we can hold on to one true constant—that God never changes. He is the same as He was in the beginning, as He will be in the end. How wonderful it is to know that He sent His only Son to be on Earth with us. Everything in creation is subject to change, and as humans, we seek stability. God tells us in Hebrews 1:10–12, "And, 'You, Lord, laid the foundation of the earth in the beginning, and the heavens are the work of your hands; they will perish, but you remain; they will all wear out like a garment, like a robe you will roll them up, like a garment they will be changed. But you are the same, and your years will have no end' " (ESV).

When relationships, jobs, and all else begin to change, we can hold on to the one true constant, God. His Word in the Bible holds truth today just as it did thousands of years ago, and as it will for all the times to come. We've all experienced change during one time or another, and maybe you're in the midst of change right now. God didn't create everything to stay the same. Seasons bring change, and we need seasons to have growth. The same goes for the changing seasons in our lives—sometimes we need to go through challenging seasons to bring forth growth.

YOU GOT THIS! *How do you handle change? When we choose to trust in Christ, we can have peace through changing times. We can be reassured that His promises never fail. He is always there for us, He always has been, and He always will be. Seek Him when changes arise and you can rest assured in His presence.*

SECOND PLACE

Be even-tempered, content with second place,
quick to forgive an offense. Forgive as quickly and completely as
the Master forgave you.

COLOSSIANS 3:13 THE MESSAGE

Competition is a part of life—between sports, grades, and more, we've all competed in some way. The prized goal is first place. We can work our hardest, practice, study, get up early to run that extra mile, and then . . . it's time to show up and second place happens. We didn't get the first-place trophy, we didn't get that A . . . or we didn't get that coveted job.

The one thing about second place versus first is that there is a goal to strive toward. When we're already in first place, we're competing to keep a title or even competing against our own record. We're reminded in Colossians to be content with second place. Take the role of the vice president, for instance. The vice president is viewed as an advisor to the number one spot, the president. But isn't this supporting role just as important as the main role? The vice president represents our country at important meetings; he or she serves as an important liaison between the administration and Congress and sometimes heads up important task forces too. Can you imagine the president trying to do all of this along with his job? Absolutely not.

We weren't made to be the best at everything individually. God gives us all unique talents and gifts. Some people will excel at one thing, whereas you will excel at another. We all need each other in this world. We need people who are the best at cooking or practicing medicine, at designing highways and teaching children. We need people who are amazing at cutting hair or producing a television show. And we need people who are skilled in supporting roles, those who will offer advice, roll up their sleeves, and remember that their work is not secondary. Our work is important to God, who placed us in our roles for a reason. And isn't it best to be where God needs us to be?

YOU GOT THIS!

Have you ever come in second place? How did it make you feel? The next time you're not placed first, remember what we learned from Colossians: supporting roles are just as important to God. When we experience times like these, it helps to have Scripture reminding us that each of our roles is important in life.

LIVING FEARLESSLY

Even though I walk through the valley of the shadow of death, I will fear no evil, for you are with me; your rod and your staff, they comfort me.

PSALM 23:4 ESV

Fear is such a strong feeling. There are times when fear can absolutely debilitate us, leaving us unable to function at our normal capacity. And even when we go to God for help and direction, sometimes our instincts automatically kick in and trigger a fight-or-flight response for the body. There are other times we fear the future and the plans He has for us. It's in these moments that we can choose to fear the unknown or choose to live fearlessly.

When you are experiencing fear of any kind, remember what God says about fear: "For God gave us a spirit not of fear but of power and love and self-control" (II Timothy 1:7 ESV).

Joshua 1:9 says, "Have I not commanded you? Be strong and courageous. Do not be frightened, and do not be dismayed, for the LORD your God is with you wherever you go" (ESV).

God reminds us throughout Scripture that He's always with us and we shouldn't fear or live with anxiety. He already has it taken care of. He knew each of us before we were born, and His plans are good.

Do you fear God's plans for you? How about asking God to give you the faith you need to trust Him? Or asking Him to erase your fears and fill your mind with His peace instead? After all, most of the things we worry about never happen. Let God's life-giving words soothe your fears.

YOU GOT THIS!

A lot of us live with fear and anxiety each day. It doesn't go away overnight. When you find yourself letting fear and anxiety creep in to situations you're struggling to deal with, remember what God wants us to know from His Word. Let His powerful words wash over you and calm you. Trying putting your trust in Him and casting your worries and fears out to sea. When you start living in His light and glory over fear, your heart and soul will be calm even in the strongest storm.

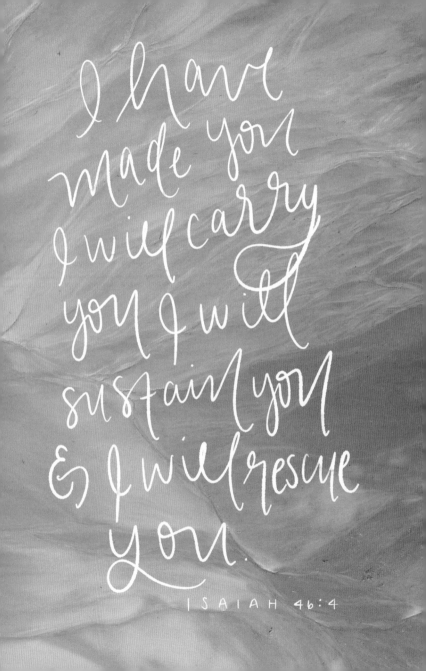

I have made you I will carry you I will sustain you & I will rescue you.

ISAIAH 46:4

ONCE I GET. . .

I have set the LORD always before me; because he is at my right hand, I shall not be shaken. Therefore my heart is glad, and my whole being rejoices; my flesh also dwells secure.

PSALM 16:8–9 ESV

Do you ever say to yourself, "Once I get [fill in the blank], then I'll be happy?" I bet many of us have thought this at one time or another. Maybe it was "once I find the one," or "once I get married," or "once I land my dream job." The problem here is that once we get whatever "it" is, we always start looking for what's next. We don't say, "Okay, I'm happy now! Never mind anything else!" We look ahead for the next thing, event, or person to make us happy.

If you're feeling that way now, ask yourself this question: What am I waiting for? You see, we're not guaranteed that thing, event, or person we're looking toward, so why not ask God to change your perspective? Ask Him to help you see the good things, events, and people already in your life. He can help you concentrate on the good that surrounds you at this very moment! You could also try looking back at all the wonderful things God has already provided in the past. When our happiness is dependent upon how others treat us or how fun the next event on our calendar is going to be, we waste our time thinking of what is to come and not enjoying what is there in the present. God wants to see you happy; He wants you to enjoy life. Ask Him to help you capture your thoughts of what might happen tomorrow and turn them into gratitude of what is happening today. He doesn't want you wasting away and waiting for something else.

It's easy to feel happy when you're reminded of whose you are: you are a daughter of God. He has amazing plans for your life even though you may not be able to see them right now. You can find happiness in knowing that you can trust the Creator of the universe with your future. We're reminded in Psalm 37:4, "Delight yourself in the LORD, and he will give you the desires of your heart" (ESV). God knows our heart and our desires. We have to trust in Him and, as we're reminded in the psalm, delight ourselves in the Lord.

YOU GOT THIS!

Allow yourself to find happiness where you are today. While we all have desires and plans for our future, our happiness comes from trusting God in every season. As humans, we naturally look to what's next. What's something you can delight in today that God has provided for you already? Let's follow the Scriptures and delight yourself in the Lord. Thank Him for what He has given you and open the desires of your heart to Him. Listen for His movement in your heart.

LIFE IS WAITING FOR YOU

But when he saw the wind, he was afraid, and beginning to sink he cried out, "Lord, save me." Jesus immediately reached out his hand and took hold of him, saying to him, "O you of little faith, why did you doubt?"

MATTHEW 14:30–31 ESV

Are you ever scared to take chances? Sometimes it's easier just to stay home with a bowl of ice cream and watch the world go by, isn't it? Maybe it's hard for you to make friends or actually do the one thing you've thought of doing, like taking a trip or joining a certain club. Maybe you've wanted to go hiking . . . or go to church again. What are you waiting for? What's holding you back? Is there something God has put on your heart to do or to be, yet it's hard for you to step out and take that chance? The nudges get stronger, but the doubt inside you grows as you think through what it might mean to put it into action.

I'm here to tell you that you are greater than you could ever imagine. God wouldn't be nudging you if He didn't think you could do it. Sometimes it's hard to get out of our comfort zones, so rather than go for it, we tend to make excuses as to why "it" can't happen. It's time to push the excuses away and start living life as God intended! Do a new thing today and step out in faith . . . get out of your comfort zone and start saying yes to the callings of your heart. It's okay to start small—maybe it's time to make that plan or put down the ice cream and open the shades a little. It's hard to do things that are new to us and sometimes even go back to things we once knew. But give yourself grace in these times and call upon the Lord to help get you where you know He wants you to be.

YOU GOT THIS!

What's been on your heart or mind lately to pursue? What's stopping you from making the next move? It can be scary to try new things and leave familiar comfort zones, but life is waiting! When we put our trust in the Lord and lean on Him for strength, we can do amazing things!

OWN PATH

Before I formed you in the womb I knew you, and before you were born I consecrated you.

JEREMIAH 1:5 ESV

Have you ever felt like you had to be the person your parents wanted you to be? Maybe you felt directed to go a certain path in life. God has created each of us to be unique and special. Yet sometimes we feel compelled to do what we went to school for or act a certain way in life.

God reminds us in Jeremiah that before you were formed in your mother's womb, He knew you. He knew His great plans for you. You don't always have to take the path that's straight ahead or of someone else's choosing; we're free in Christ to walk the path He calls us to. It may not be what you went to school for or what you or your parents dreamed up, but it's your own! Allow yourself to pivot in life and veer to the path less traveled. Sometimes we don't even know the amazing things God has equipped us with until we're faced with new adventures and challenges.

We can get blinded by seeing others' paths and wanting their lives or what they have, but it's best to stay on our own. The grass isn't always greener over there. Don't wish away your amazing gifts, talents, and plan for someone else's. You are worthy, and your story was perfectly created by the Father.

YOU GOT THIS! *Have you ever felt like you had to take a certain path in life? God created your own path to be unique. No matter your circumstances, your past, or what you've done, He has a good plan for you! It's okay to take a different direction than what you thought you'd do originally. Take the leap of faith and trust in Him to venture into the unknown!*

YOUR GIFTS

As each has received a gift, use it to serve one another, as good stewards of God's varied grace: whoever speaks, as one who speaks oracles of God; whoever serves, as one who serves by the strength that God supplies—in order that in everything God may be glorified through Jesus Christ. To him belong glory and dominion forever and ever. Amen.

I PETER 4:10–11 ESV

Did you know you have special gifts? How wonderful is that? First Corinthians 12:4–6 says, "There are different kinds of spiritual gifts, but the same Spirit is the source of them all. There are different kinds of service, but we serve the same Lord. God works in different ways, but it is the same God who does the work in all of us" (NLT).

Have you ever wondered what your gifts are? Sometimes it's easier to see the gifts God has given to others, isn't it? But I bet others can see your gifts! When negative thoughts start to creep in, like "Her gift is better than mine," think again. Think about what you love to do and truly enjoy. Maybe it's something you do every day and don't even realize it. Like we learned in I Peter, we are to use our gifts to serve one another. I'm sure you know someone who is an amazing cook and another who gives of their time and another with a great ear for listening. Friend, let me tell you today: the gifts God gave you are powerful, and they have the potential to be world-changing. God's power is as strong in you as it is in anyone else. All you have to do is tap into it.

YOU GOT THIS!

What special gifts do you have? Are you not sure what gifts He has given you? Ask Him! God will help you identify the unique gifts He has placed in you. Ask Him to show you where and how and when to use them, and then watch as His power shines through you in the most amazing ways. Remember, it's all in His timing. No matter where you are in your spiritual journey, your gifts are important and will be used in amazing ways!

GIVING THANKS

*Giving thanks always and for everything to God the Father
in the name of our Lord Jesus Christ.*

EPHESIANS 5:20 ESV

Life keeps us busy. As women, we always have a thousand tabs open in our brains. Yet somehow we keep it all together (most of the time). We pray about the things we need, but when God answers our prayers or has different plans, do we stop to give thanks? We are reminded in Ephesians to give thanks always and to give thanks for everything—and by everything, that means whether things go our way or not. The truth is that His plan isn't always our plan and our tracks don't always align. But even if they don't, that doesn't mean He's not working all things out for our good. Trust me, there will be times when your faith is tested and on trial. But it's in these times that we can find peace by leaning on God and fully trusting Him with our lives, goals, and dreams.

Just think—maybe that relationship didn't work out because God was saving you from a toxic situation. Maybe you were late to a meeting because He was saving you from a car accident. Maybe He wants you to stay in your current role instead of moving up the ladder because He knows the positions that will be in jeopardy during the next round of layoffs. We can't see the bigger picture, but God can. So the next time you feel like He dropped the ball, think about all the things God could be saving you from—and give thanks.

YOU GOT THIS!

Take a moment to just be. Let everything God is doing for you now come to mind—the answered and unanswered prayers. Take time now to surrender to Him and His great plans for you. When we remind ourselves that He's in control, our anxieties and worries release. The next time your prayers are answered—or even when you step outside—be surrounded by His beauty and stay thankful for His diligent work in your life.

LIVING WATER

He turns rivers into a desert,
springs of water into thirsty ground.

PSALM 107:33 ESV

God is good. He is in control. When our souls are dry, He fills us with living water. John 4:13–15, 24 says, "Jesus said to her, 'Everyone who drinks of this water will be thirsty again, but whoever drinks of the water that I will give him will never be thirsty again. The water that I will give him will become in him a spring of water welling up to eternal life.' The woman said to him, 'Sir, give me this water, so that I will not be thirsty or have to come here to draw water.' . . . 'God is spirit, and those who worship him must worship in spirit and truth.' "

There are times when we have dry spots in life . . . in marriage . . . in work. . . . However, during these times, it's important that we remember to turn to Jesus for the life-giving water that only He provides. If you're in a dry spot today, why not ask Jesus to refresh your soul and renew your heart? And as He fills your heart with fresh hope, take time to sit in His presence, to feel His peace, and to worship His Name. When we quiet ourselves before God and worship Him in spirit and in truth, the shower that washes over the soul is life-altering. Sometimes it's hard to be fully present during worship. Sometimes we have too many things on our mind, or maybe we haven't been to church in years. The good news is, you can worship anytime and anywhere. Remember, His well never runs dry.

YOU GOT THIS! *Whether in times of drought or prosperity, you can always be refreshed with the Living Water Jesus provides. He loves you more than you could ever imagine. He desires you to seek Him and be filled with His love, grace, and mercy. Are you in a time of drought, joy, despair, or hope? No matter where you are, Jesus is with you! Seek Him today and every day.*

GRACE AND MERCY

There is no fear in love, but perfect love casts out fear. For fear has to do with punishment, and whoever fears has not been perfected in love. We love because he first loved us.

I JOHN 4:18–19 ESV

We've all "messed up" before. As humans, we are not perfect. And because of this, we tend to think we're not worthy of God's love. We think our past is too much for God's love and mercy. Or we think we're not good enough to be forgiven for the not-so-great strongholds that keep us from living a life worthy of God's love. Friends, let me tell you something—these are all lies we tell ourselves. The truth is, Jesus loves you! His grace and mercy are so great. You don't have to fear Him.

Sometimes we can feel as if we're not worthy to step into church or to even pray. It's so easy to let these falsities take over our lives. But Jesus wants you just the way you are. His perfect love washes away fear. Instead of letting the lies take root, why not ask God to help you see the truth? You'll find that He is so loving. He wants you to bring all your fears and troubles to Him. He hasn't forgotten about you. He's always been there for you, and He always will be there. When you're falling apart, reach out to God and let Him hold you in His hands. Release your fear and let His faithfulness wash over you. He is bigger than the circumstances you are facing. His plan is perfect. God doesn't want you to punish yourself or feel like you're not good enough for Him. He knew you before you were born and He loves you just as you are!

YOU GOT THIS!

Do you ever feel like you're not good enough to come to the One Most High? He is accepting you with open arms. Whether you're upset, scared, fearful, or joyful, He desires you! Let His presence wash over you and watch your fears disappear.

I NEED YOU, JESUS

Anxiety in a man's heart weighs him down,
but a good word makes him glad.

PROVERBS 12:25 ESV

Have you ever been weighed down by anxiety? Maybe you planned an event for months only to get stuck in traffic when the big day arrives . . . or maybe work is piling up and you feel overwhelmed. Maybe all the dishes are dirty and you just want to get a glass of water but everything else has to come first. Anxiety is a part of our daily lives whether we like it or not. It comes in small and big waves in our best and worst moments. When you start to feel your shoulders tensing up, try to remember that you have a release tactic—leaning on Jesus. One way to stop anxiety in its tracks is to recite favorite Scripture verses or hum a favorite worship song. This always brings me back to what matters most.

Also, breathe. It's okay to not have everything work out the exact way you've planned it. It's okay to not know the answer to what will happen next. It's okay to let the dishes wait. It's okay to arrive late for a meeting. It's okay to not agree with everyone, and it's okay to not let others' opinions of you weigh on your soul. We can and we will disappoint people, but how does disappointing people compare to disappointing Jesus? Here is a big truth bomb for you: why be anxious when God, the One who sees your future, is working through and in all things for His great plan? When you are anxious for the future, lean on Him. Let Him know you need Him—in both the small worries and the big concerns. And He will give you a peace beyond all understanding.

YOU GOT THIS! *Do you have any favorite Scriptures you can lean on when you feel anxious? Jeremiah 29:11 is a great go-to: "For I know the plans I have for you, declares the LORD, plans for welfare and not for evil, to give you a future and a hope" (ESV). He has a special purpose and future for you. Don't let anxiety overwhelm you. Instead, whisper God's Word and allow His fresh hope to wash over you!*

SPEAK TRUTH

The good person out of the good treasure of his heart produces good, and the evil person out of his evil treasure produces evil, for out of the abundance of the heart his mouth speaks.

Do you know any of these kinds of people—the "Debbie Downers," the "Everything Is Wrong-ers," or even the "Everything Is Great-ers"? How is your own soul? Is it filled with the light of Jesus, or is it down about things that happen in life? Sometimes it's hard for us to accept that His plans are different from ours, and when we don't get that promotion or new job or succeed at mastering that new interest, we can really get disappointed. We see the doors that God closed for us as missed opportunities or unanswered prayers. But maybe the unanswered prayers were actually answered in a way you never dreamed and will never understand—only God knows.

The sad part is that when we feel defeated by what we think are "missed opportunities," we tend to pour out our negative feelings onto those around us. It's true. When the heart is filled with God's love, we attract the good in the people around us. When we're in this healthy state, people want to be around us because they are drawn to the light. However, when we fill the heart with negativity, it spills over in what we say. And we start attracting the darkness in people around us. When we speak the truth, our heart is filled with the light and love of Jesus. When we focus on the negative, well, negativity is exactly what we get and give.

What will you build your life and soul upon? How will you choose to respond to life's circumstances? When we're down, it's easy for us to start believing that we're not good enough and we forget about the great things God has in store for us. Is your heart filled with negativity today? If so, can you pinpoint the reason why you are feeling this way? Once you recognize the pain point, ask God to help you walk through your feelings of negativity and disappointment. He wants all of you—and that includes the hard, not-so-beautiful stuff. Ask Him to fill you with His light so that you can reflect it to those around you.

YOU GOT THIS! *Do a soul check. What is your soul filled with, positivity or negativity? When you face situations, do you find yourself tracking in a downward spiral—feeling bad for yourself and filling your soul with negativity? Lean on Jesus and begin to fill your soul with good treasure to produce even more good through Him.*

THE GUIDE

This is the day that the LORD has made;
let us rejoice and be glad in it.

PSALM 118:24 ESV

Each day is never the same, even when it feels like it is. Sometimes we write our plans in our planners, hoping to cross off our lists. Then we get interrupted by life. Maybe our kids need us or a friend gives us a call or we have to run to the store because there's just nothing in the house to eat for dinner. It seems as if our days always get disrupted by one thing or another. These changes cause us to become unsettled. We become upset that our day wasn't as productive as we had initially planned. And instead of focusing on what we did accomplish, we tend to focus on what didn't get done.

Here's an idea: every morning, surrender your daily plan to God. Invite Him to create little interruptions, as these can be blessings in disguise. Maybe you'll run into an old friend while at the store or think of a new business plan while driving or get a call from your friend with wonderful news. Oh! And the kids in your life— whether it be your son or daughter or nephew or niece or grandchildren, remember—they grow up fast! Ask God to provide moments for you to enjoy them. Ask Him to open your eyes today. Even when the sun doesn't shine, it always comes up. God wants us to be glad in the work He gives us each day; He doesn't want us to focus on tasks that take away our happiness. Accept the little changes in the day—even the big ones! Grant yourself the freedom and the grace to enjoy each day, however God lays it out for you.

YOU GOT THIS! *Do you plan out your days before they even start? How do you feel when your plans are interrupted or don't come through? It's hard giving up this control, but when we surrender to God's plans for us, we can ask Him to help us see the joy in each day instead of focusing on our to-do list. Today, why not welcome the little disruptions? And don't forget to thank God for the day that He made.*

be the
girl who
decided to
go for it

A PERFECT WORLD

*For I consider that the sufferings of this present time
are not worth comparing with the glory that is to be
revealed to us.*

ROMANS 8:18 ESV

Imagine a different life, a different world, where everything went as perfectly as planned with no sickness, no hurt, and no pain. Would you still need God? We often go to God when we need something. Having an easy, perfect life doesn't call on a "need" for God. Often, trials and tribulations bring us closer to Him. We learn that we can lean on Him when we don't have His understanding of what we're going through. We've learned that we should always come to Him in good times and in hard times.

Have you ever lifted weights? Lifting causes damage to your muscles, building them up stronger than they were before. That is what can happen when we learn to come to God. We're torn down, only to be built back up by the Lord and come out of the pain stronger than before. Our roots grow deeper, so when storms arise, we're ready—standing strong in God's armor as the wind whips the trees around.

We don't live in a perfect world. When the storms, the trials, the tribulations come, the only way to remain steadfast and strong, ready to face whatever comes to us, is by tapping into God's strength. By equipping ourselves with Scripture, we can stand on a solid foundation, knowing that God's plans far outweigh the storms. When the winds pick up, we stand strong. It's not always easy; in fact, we've all let the storm blow us around in the past. But the next time you sense a storm coming on, ask God to cover you in His peace and then let the clouds pass as you remain unshakable.

YOU GOT THIS!

God is chasing after you. He is the light of the world even when it seems too dark. We don't live in a perfect world, but we live in God's perfect will and plan for us. Let His strength wash over you and build you so that you will be fully prepared for whatever comes your way.

LISTEN BEFORE
SPEAKING

*Know this, my beloved brothers: let every person
be quick to hear, slow to speak, slow to anger.*

JAMES 1:19 ESV

How often have we waited for someone to stop speaking so we could talk? And vice versa—I'm sure you've spoken with a friend or colleague and knew the person wasn't listening. Rather, they were waiting to speak their views. How did that feel? Did you feel heard? We've all been there, so don't feel alone. God teaches us to be slow to speak and to truly listen to what others are saying. We are to make sure that others feel heard and understood. When we speak over others or want them to wrap up what they are saying just so we can talk about ourselves, we aren't truly holding a great conversation.

The last part of James 1:19 says to be slow to anger. How do you feel about this? Do you practice it? It's not easy—especially when we're in a passionate argument and we just know we're right. I mean, in the heat of the moment, are we supposed to not react? Are we just supposed to walk away? That does seem to be exactly what James is saying—take a breath and respond with love. When talking with someone we don't agree with, listen to what they are saying and talk through it so that where they're coming from is better understood.

Instead of hearing one piece of what they're saying and allowing it to flare us quickly to anger, think before reacting and retorting. I'm not saying it's easy; it definitely takes practice.

We're reminded in Proverbs 18:2, "A fool takes no pleasure in understanding, but only in expresing his opinion" (ESV). Think about the last argument you were in. Did stating your differing opinion solve anything? Did it change the other person's viewpoint? Probably not. When you find yourself in a heated argument, try to think of this verse in James and be slow to anger. God wants us to be good to one another and to forgive each another. Try to remember that God made us all unique with different ideas and individual gifts for a reason.

YOU GOT THIS!

The next time you're talking with someone, don't overthink it! Keep it simple—listen to what they have to say, be slow to respond, and don't be quick to get angry. Do you find yourself pushing your views over having a great conversation? Let the other person be heard, understand what they're saying, and be slow to speak. Try it! I'm sure you'll find it was worth your while. Who knows? You may even get your point across for the very first time.

LEADING

Don't be selfish; don't try to impress others. Be humble,
thinking of others as better than yourselves.

PHILIPPIANS 2:3 NLT

Are you a leader or a follower? Do you like to take action and make plans, or do you like for plans and decisions to be laid out before you? In today's world, the term *leader* is often described as someone with *manager, CEO,* or *director* in their title, but the truth is, people don't have to be in high-level positions to lead. Often in jobs, bosses look for their team members to lead in their individual roles. It helps relieve the boss from all the things they have to do and decide, saving them time and energy.

Whether you just landed your first job or have been in your role for years, think about some ways you can lead others and impact your company. Do you have an idea for a different department? Why not run it by them? Remember, you're not working for you or for the company; you're working for the Lord, with a God-given purpose.

You can lead outside of the workplace too. At home, you can lead with your actions. A true leader steps in when they see others struggling. Is your husband super busy this week? Are your kids struggling to manage their time between homework, chores, and extracurricular activities? Make a plan to simplify your home life and present it to your husband and kids. God made you unique; He gave you creative ideas and good solutions. Even if your title doesn't include the word *manager* it doesn't mean that you are not called to see the bigger picture, to share your thoughts, and to lead your team and your home to new ground . . . ground that would never be thought of without you.

YOU GOT THIS!

When He walked the earth, Jesus gave us a great example of what a leader looks like. How can you resemble Jesus in your everyday life? If you're not sure where you should start, pray to see where and how you can become a helpful servant to those around you.

BE STRONG AND SPEAK UP

But by the grace of God I am what I am, and his grace toward me
was not in vain. On the contrary, I worked harder than any of them,
though it was not I, but the grace of God that is with me.

I CORINTHIANS 15:10 ESV

Have you ever had an idea but didn't think anyone really wanted to hear it? As women, we often feel unheard because we've been told we live in a "man's world." Some of us don't feel comfortable negotiating for a raise or buying a new car because we feel like a man should do those things instead. Why do we feel this way? Is it really beyond us to work out a deal that is beneficial to both parties? Perhaps you are competing against other women to be heard at the boardroom table. What's holding you back? What would happen if you voiced your opinion?

Believe it or not, we actually don't have to change who we are to get more comfortable with standing up for ourselves. It's not about being more manly or thinking like a man—you're the strong woman God made you to be! It's about being confident in who God made you to be and knowing that you are strong and courageous just the way you are! It doesn't matter where you came from; it only matters where you're going. Stay strong in your faith and ask God for the words and the confidence to speak up.

We're reminded in Psalm 46:5, "God is in the midst of her; she shall not be moved; God will help her when morning dawns" (ESV). The Bible is full of women who are strong! In Proverbs 31:10–31, the Bible talks of a woman who fears the Lord. Verses 16–17 and 25–26 say, "She considers a field and buys it; with the fruit of her hands she plants a vineyard. She dresses herself with strength and makes her arms strong. . . . Strength and dignity are her clothing, and she laughs at the time to come. She opens her mouth with wisdom, and the teaching of kindness is on her tongue" (ESV). God doesn't want us to just sit back and not show what we have to give to the world and others. Be strong!

(Maybe you feel absolutely comfortable with speaking up, voicing your opinion, and negotiating deals. If so, think about reaching out to other women in your circle and encouraging them to be bold. Sometimes all we need is a little push to feel comfortable enough to share our thoughts!)

YOU GOT THIS!

Do not be afraid. You are strong and courageous! Let the strength God has provided you to shine through! You can do anything God has called you to do through Christ! When you get those great ideas, don't be afraid to speak. Hold true to yourself. Have faith in you!

TRUST FALL

The LORD is my shepherd; I shall not want. He makes me lie down in green pastures. He leads me beside still waters. He restores my soul. He leads me in paths of righteousness for his name's sake. Even though I walk through the valley of the shadow of death, I will fear no evil, for you are with me; your rod and your staff, they comfort me.

PSALM 23:1–4 ESV

Do you remember attempting the famous "trust fall" with your friends when you were a kid? It was so hard, wasn't it? I was always standing there thinking, "Will they still be behind me, or will they let me fall flat on the ground?" If we transition that idea to adulthood, perhaps you've wondered about letting go and doing a trust fall with Jesus. The answer—and best news—is that He will be there to catch you. We don't have to worry! If we give it all to God—all our circumstances, our worries, our hopes, and our dreams—rest assured, He is always with us. Want even more good news? He's already aware of all that ails us! And He's working in and through every circumstance, not just yours. That's right, even though it's hard to believe, God's not just working in your life; He's working in billions of lives all over the globe. What an amazing thought! So when we ask for something and the answer isn't what we'd desire, we have to remember that if we did get what we asked for, it could change the course of His plan and affect others. All our lives are intertwined and connected whether we realize it or not.

We're reminded in Psalm 23 not to fear because He's always with us! Let His rod and staff comfort you. When you surrender and fall into the hands of Jesus, let Him guide your life for good! Unanswered prayers and circumstances can be okay in your soul because you know that God is in control.

YOU GOT THIS!

Today, you can give up control. Do a trust fall with Jesus and know He's there behind you. Remember that He's got you in the palms of His hands. We are serving a faithful God who knows so much more than we could ever imagine, and He is working in and through all things. The next time you try to depend merely on your own understanding, take a humble stance and remember, God's got this, so you've got this!

BE REMINDED

Do not love the world or the things in the world. If anyone loves the world, the love of the Father is not in him.

I JOHN 2:15 ESV

When we don't get the answers we cry out for, doubt can set in pretty quickly. We've all had times when we wanted certain things to happen but didn't get the results we were hoping for. Maybe we've wanted our prayers to be answered in a specific way and they weren't. When we feel that God has failed us, it's easy to let thoughts of this world creep into our minds—thoughts of doubt, resentment, and failure. But those thoughts are not from God. Those thoughts will try to pull you away from Jesus and lessen your trust in Him. When you feel your mind leading you down this path, pull back! Remember, He's a waymaker, a miracle worker, and a promise keeper.

Throughout Scripture, we are told not to conform to the world we live in. The world can suck us in and cause us to lose sight of the One Most High. When we are in dark places, He is the light of the world. God never stops working for us! When we feel He has failed us, we just have to wait—what He has planned is so much greater than we could ever imagine. Our lives won't always work out how we'd like them to, but if we continue to give it all to God, He will make it okay. The truth is, we were never promised an easy life. But we were promised a life filled with God's joy, strength, courage, peace, and grace. He is full of so much goodness! God has never left you, He never has, and He never will.

YOU GOT THIS!

Sometimes we need a good reminder of Jesus's love for us. Our desires and wants and dreams sometimes don't align with God's plan for us. And His plan is better than anything we could dream up! While it's easy to give up when we don't get our way, let's not allow our disappointments to turn into doubt or other worldly thoughts. When we rely on Jesus instead of the world, we can live in much greater peace and understanding.

SERVE LIKE JESUS

For even the Son of Man came not to be served but to serve, and to give his life as a ransom for many.

MARK 10:45 ESV

Jesus isn't just about salvation; He is also about restoration. His work didn't stop at the cross. His mission isn't simply about wiping away our sins and securing our place in heaven. It's also about calling us into a new life altogether— one that He can continue to work through. We're called to have a heart like Jesus.

We're reminded in Ephesians 2:10, "For we are his workmanship, created in Christ Jesus for good works, which God prepared beforehand, that we should walk in them" (ESV). We're called and enabled to do the great things that God has planned for each one of us.

Mark 10:45 has us recall that Jesus came from a powerful position, yet He showed humility. Let's live like Jesus did! Are you in a powerful position? Act humbly. Jesus didn't want the glory; He gave it back to the One who sent Him, His Father, God.

Lastly, Matthew 28:18–20 states, "And Jesus came and said to them, 'All authority in heaven and on earth has been given to me. Go therefore and make disciples of all nations, baptizing them in the name of the Father and of the Son and of the Holy Spirit, teaching them to observe all that I have commanded you. And behold, I am with you always, to the end of the age'" (ESV). Jesus is always with us, guiding us to lead with a servant's heart.

YOU GOT THIS!

The next time you seek forgiveness, let restoration take place in your soul—let Him give you a new life! And remember to live as Jesus did. When we make us less and Him more, we help build His kingdom for good, and that is the ultimate goal.

MAKING A DIFFERENCE

For even the Son of Man came not to be served but to serve
others and to give his life as a ransom for many.

MARK 10:45 NLT

Sometimes we pour our heart into certain projects and endeavors only to feel as if the outcome didn't really make a difference. But maybe that's not the case! What if the work we finished hasn't yet yielded its crop? Does that mean we should give up the work we're doing? No! God can work in and through you to accomplish His will for the world. Things we do today may not take effect for many years to come, and we have to be okay with not knowing how our actions will impact the future. Having faith means being okay while not seeing the final results.

As humans, we like to see things finished. We make bread and we want to eat it after it's done or we take a test and want to know our grade. What if we removed ourselves from an outcome and simply focused on the task at hand? What if we decided to have faith in the fact that what we're doing today will make a difference? It may not matter tomorrow or the next day or even next month—but it will in the years, decades, and maybe even centuries to come. It's amazing how one life can touch more lives and the goodness can spread like wildfire.

Even if you're not sure what difference you can make, know that your actions can be as small as offering help to a neighbor—there's no need to travel the globe or do something profound!. Let Jesus's light shine through you in all you do. If you humbly touch another's heart in a positive way, you are serving them. If you are listening to God's little nudges, serving those around you, and taking on the tasks He's placed before you, you will yield fruit. You can trust that!

YOU GOT THIS!

Sometimes serving causes us to get out of our comfort zones. We're unsure of how others will react or whether what we're doing will actually make a difference. The good news is, any good work is not for nothing. Instead of looking for the "thank you," look at what it can do to grow the kingdom over your pride. When we live humbly and act like Jesus, we can and will make a difference, no matter how big or how small our efforts are.

HOW WILL YOU SOW?

The point is this: whoever sows sparingly will also reap sparingly, and whoever sows bountifully will also reap bountifully. Each one must give as he has decided in his heart, not reluctantly or under compulsion, for God loves a cheerful giver. And God is able to make all grace abound to you, so that having all sufficiency in all things at all times, you may abound in every good work. As it is written, "He has distributed freely, he has given to the poor; his righteousness endures forever."

II CORINTHIANS 9:6–9 ESV

Remember your first paycheck? When we got that first job and finally saw a paycheck, we felt so great about actually getting money for working! Did your mom or dad teach you about saving money—or tell you to start putting it away for retirement when you were in your early 20s? Many of us can remember being at church and hearing tithing messages. As soon as the pastor spoke we thought, *I worked so hard for this money, and I need it to pay bills. . . . I'm not sure what I should or can give.*

Money is a tough subject, and it can be difficult to decide what to give or keep. We learn in Proverbs 23:4–5, "Do not toil to acquire wealth; be discerning enough to desist. When your eyes light on it, it is gone, for suddenly it sprouts wings, flying like an eagle toward heaven" (ESV). What we have to remember is that our money isn't truly ours, it's God's. When we give, it is multiplied to further His kingdom beyond our measure. When we give, we should do so without being reluctant or feeling compelled. We must give freely from our heart—as much or as little as we feel fit.

YOU GOT THIS! *Where is your heart today? How do you feel about the money you make? It's always good to save, as we never know when we will have to dig into our savings to fix a leaking roof or a car repair bill. How do you feel about tithing? When we tithe, we put our money into a different kind of account—an account that will keep growing dividends and expand beyond our measure.*

NO TIME FOR THIS

I am the true vine, and my Father is the vinedresser.
Every branch in me that does not bear fruit he takes away, and
every branch that does bear fruit he prunes, that it may bear more
fruit. Already you are clean because of the word that I have spoken
to you. Abide in me, and I in you. As the branch cannot bear fruit
by itself, unless it abides in the vine, neither can you, unless you
abide in me. I am the vine; you are the branches. Whoever abides
in me and I in him, he it is that bears much fruit, for apart from
me you can do nothing.

JOHN 15:1–5 ESV

It seems that when our lives become too busy, everything comes crashing down on us. We're running full steam ahead, marking off our mile-long to-do lists, and then bam!—an unexpected life change happens. Whether it's a friend who turned on you or your boss telling you that your position is being moved out of state, it's never easy when change hits so abruptly. And it leaves us thinking, *How in the world will I be able to face this?*

God never promised that our days would go smoothly or exactly how we planned. In fact, He said the complete opposite in John 16:33: "In this world you will have trouble" (NIV). When you're up against a hard life transition or life feels out of control, try to remember one thing: God's got this! We try to control so much of our lives that when things beyond our control or things we didn't plan for happen, it causes us to wonder whether everything will be okay.

The next time you start questioning the outcome, remember this simple three-step process. Step 1: Surrender. Step 2: Know that you are in good hands. Step 3: Be okay with not knowing why a new path has appeared beneath your feet and know that you can trust Jesus. He has a plan for it! He may not want you to have those particular friends in your life anymore. Maybe a move is so your children will attend a different school and meet certain people who will make a huge impact on their lives. The reasons are endless and so complex that we have to humbly surrender and know that we will never understand (on this earth) "why" God works in the ways He does.

YOU GOT THIS!

How do you feel when life-altering changes suddenly take place? The next time you come to a crossroads in life, humbly surrender and be okay with the new path God wants you to take. Nothing ever stays the same—we can be certain of that. But we can also be certain that His plans are good!

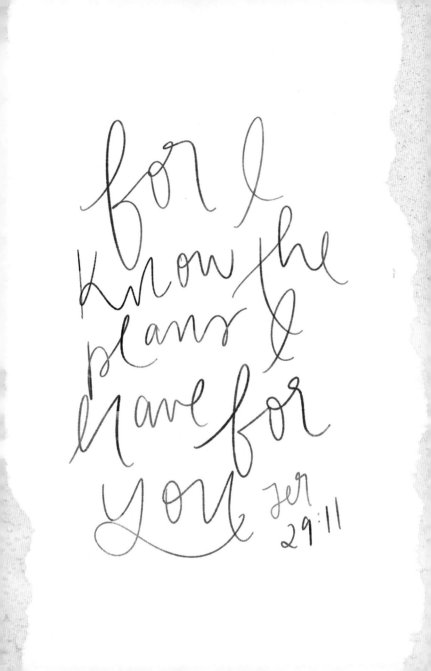

YOU ARE THE SALT

You are the salt of the earth, but if salt has lost its taste, how shall its saltiness be restored? It is no longer good for anything except to be thrown out and trampled under people's feet. You are the light of the world. A city set on a hill cannot be hidden. Nor do people light a lamp and put it under a basket, but on a stand, and it gives light to all in the house. In the same way, let your light shine before others, so that they may see your good works and give glory to your Father who is in heaven.

MATTHEW 5:13–16 ESV

You may be thinking, I'm salt? Back in Jesus's time, salt was a prized commodity. It was used to preserve food (as there was no refrigeration); it was rich in minerals being mined from the Dead Sea; and it was used to heal wounds. As salt, we are part of the healing and preservation. Salt is effective when it's used—either sprinkled or rubbed into food or put into the wound. To be the salt, we have to come in contact with those who need it—to heal their wounds and offer hope through Jesus. This is where our story comes into play. God has placed certain people on our path to touch our lives and for us to touch their lives. Telling our story of how we came to know Jesus can be hard. We can doubt that our story isn't good enough, or we can be unsure of how people will respond. Maybe we're too scared to share with others what has happened in our lives. We can't secure others' salvation; that's up to God. What we can do is share how God has worked in our lives and share our story with those who listen. After all, we are where we are for a reason.

YOU GOT THIS!

Who can you share your story with? It may be in person or even online. It's amazing how many people need to hear your story; there are always similarities when stories are shared in groups. There, we don't feel alone, and we can find others who have gone through similar experiences. Then we can help lift up each other! God wants to work through you, and He wants you to share your story so that you can preserve what is good and be a light in the world!

STANDING FIRM

For we do not wrestle against flesh and blood, but against the rulers, against the authorities, against the cosmic powers over this present darkness, against the spiritual forces of evil in the heavenly places.

EPHESIANS 6:12 ESV

We are in a battle, a battle against good and evil, every day of our lives. The Bible tells us to "Be sober-minded; be watchful. Your adversary the devil prowls around like a roaring lion, seeking someone to devour" (I Peter 5:8 ESV). Every day, we're in a war zone. And we have an enemy who is trying to pull us away from God and what is good. The evil one makes false promises, and he wants us to think of what matters in this world, not what matters to God. The enemy is unfortunately very good at this! He causes confusion and chaos, and before we know it, we can feel attacked on all fronts and choose to travel the wrong path—a path that feels as if waves are closing in on us. During these times, we start to wonder where God is. Are you trapped on this downward spiral today? If so, you're not alone! So many of us have fallen for the evil one's tricks. The good news is, we already know who wins the war. God does! .

When I feel under attack, I look to Ephesians 6:11–17 NIV, where it says, "Put on the full armor of God, so that you can take your stand against the devil's schemes. For our struggle is not against flesh and blood, but against the rulers, against the authorities, against the powers of this dark world and against the spiritual forces of evil in the heavenly realms. Therefore put on the full armor of God, so that when the day of evil comes, you may be able to stand your ground, and after you have done everything, to stand. Stand firm then, with the belt of truth buckled around your waist, with the breastplate of righteousness in place, and with your feet fitted with the readiness that comes from the gospel of peace. In addition to all this, take up the shield of faith, with which you can extinguish all the flaming arrows of the evil one. Take the helmet of salvation and the sword of the Spirit, which is the word of God." Close your eyes and picture yourself in this armor—the belt, the breastplate, holding a shield—and know that the One who has already won the war loves you, will never leave you, and longs to give you all the joy, strength, and hope you need to live a peaceful life.

YOU GOT THIS!

When you come under attack, remember the armor of God. Sometimes the evil one can be so sly that we don't even know we're in battle. He knows our weaknesses and is really good at talking us out of the truth we know. Instead of falling into his hands, take up your sword and be ready for the fight, standing your ground with the belt of truth and the breastplate of righteousness.

LIFTING OTHERS UP

As iron sharpens iron, so a friend sharpens a friend.

PROVERBS 27:17 NLT

What does your friend group look like? What about a small group—do you feel connected with other believers outside of church? When we have community, we have others to lean on when things don't go as planned, people who will celebrate the wins with us.. When we need to be lifted up, our friends in our community can be the ones to hold us up. We're not meant to go through life alone or deal with each new problem by ourselves. As we're reminded in Proverbs 27:17, a friend sharpens a friend. When we have friends who also follow Jesus, they can remind us of His goodness when we need it most. It goes the other way too. We can be a good friend to others by giving them warm reminders of God's love and an ear to listen. Is there someone at work who eats lunch alone? Can you invite a neighbor to your next girls' night? You never know who needs a friend or community to help them and guide them along the way.

Are you looking for a trusted community? Sometimes it can be scary to join a small group at church—especially if you don't know anyone in it. But they are often the best places to form long-lasting friendships. And they are people you can rely on for prayer or to lend a helping hand or to be a good, true friend.

YOU GOT THIS! *What does your community look like? Have you ever considered joining a small group at church? If you aren't connected yet, there are online communities through social media. It's amazing to be connected with other like-minded women, whether they're just starting their walk with Christ or have years of experience in studying the Scriptures. No matter where you are in your journey, you're accepted just as you are!*

BEING AUTHENTIC

It's who you are and the way you live that count before God. Your worship must engage your spirit in the pursuit of truth. That's the kind of people the Father is out looking for: those who are simply and honestly themselves before Him in their worship. God is sheer being itself—Spirit. Those who worship Him must do it out of their very being, their spirits, their true selves, in adoration.

JOHN 4:23-24 THE MESSAGE

Do you ever simply go through the motions when it comes to prayer? Being busy women, we usually have a thousand things running through our heads—grocery lists, to-do lists, concerns at work, what we're going to make for dinner—and before we know it, we've completely forgotten that we were even talking to God. The next time you're praying, try to surrender all your thoughts to Him. You can even ask Him to clear your mind and help you be fully present.

Have you ever been watching your kids on the playground and then out of nowhere a big important meeting from work takes over your thoughts? What happens next? You miss the opportunity to play with your kids! Maybe you've been at work and couldn't stop thinking about what your husband said the night before. How are you supposed to concentrate on the task at hand when all you can think about is how you should have responded?

By finding a quiet place and time to be present with God, you are giving yourself the best gift you could ever ask for. It takes practice and patience to control your mind and not let it wander. When you find a thought creeping in about work or the kids, why not write it down and think about it later? Or if it's not needed in the moment, ask God to help you dismiss it so you can turn your focus back to Him. Whether you're at home or work, invite God to be at the forefront of your focus. Wherever you are and whatever you're doing, be one hundred percent in that moment with Him. It won't always be perfect or easy, but when we can give the attention to Him, we can be fully there rather than just going through the motions.

YOU GOT THIS!

The next time you're praying, see what comes to mind. Is your mind filled with everything else? I know it's hard, but what if we closed all the "tabs" we have open in our minds and concentrated instead on the people in front of us and the God who loves us. When we're with our families, friends, or at work, see how many distractions come to mind. Take notice and write down actions to take on later, focusing on what's important in that moment.

TAKING TIME AWAY

Create in me a clean heart, O God, and renew a right spirit within me. Cast me not away from your presence, and take not your Holy Spirit from me. Restore to me the joy of your salvation, and uphold me with a willing spirit.

PSALM 51:10–12 ESV

As women, we spend a lot of time working, being in school, being a mom, and so much more. We make sure the kids are taken care of and make sure there's food in the fridge . . . our days are filled to the brim. We often put the lives of others before ours and even forget about ourselves. There are not many moments for "me" time, especially as our plates get fuller and fuller. But we too need restoration of the soul and mind to be the best wives, moms, workers, sisters, daughters, friends that we can. Every woman has different responsibilities, in and outside of the home, but the one thing holds true—we need to remember us too. We often put ourselves last, but when we're weighed down by that, we need time for ourselves.

Whether you choose to just sit outside and be or dig into the Word or stare up at the stars, take some time to find you again. Taking time for yourself can be so refreshing, wholesome, and wonderful. It may only happen for a few moments each week, but maybe that's all you need for your soul to be renewed.

Sometimes it's hard to find the time. What would happen if you started waking up a little earlier to spend a time with God? Or maybe you'd rather go to bed late and sit in His presence as you look deep into the night sky? If you are alone each day, I hear you too! The hardest time for me was when I lived alone—I felt like I had too much alone time. If you feel this way, pray and ask God to reveal where you can serve to share your gifts with others. No matter where you are in your journey, always make sure you have some time for you.

YOU GOT THIS!

It's okay to take time away. This is such a hard concept to grasp when we feel like there's no time left for us, but we're allowed to step away and have "me" time, even if it's only a 15-minute break. You can go back to what you were doing feeling renewed and refreshed. Think about it: what would you enjoy doing? When can you give yourself some time to just be? Maybe set some "me" time up for tomorrow—even mark it down. Make it happen, for you!

FILLING THE VOID

For though I am absent in body, yet I am with you in spirit, rejoicing to see your good order and the firmness of your faith in Christ.

COLOSSIANS 2:5 ESV

Phones and social media are part of a topic of much discussion these days. New media platforms pop up and others leave. Good news and bad news are sent worldwide in an instant. We hear people's opinions immediately. It's a different world than the one we knew growing up, for sure.

When we do have a few moments to ourselves during our busy days, we can find ourselves mindlessly scrolling through Instagram or Facebook. We are all guilty of it—even kids love watching shows on YouTube. We often think we are just going to quickly look up one thing, but before we know it, we've taken ten quizzes to try to figure out which cat we are most like. It's true! And while we scroll, we are mentally registering all the "great times" others are having. But even when we go out to eat to make our own "great time," people are glued to their phones with no true conversation to be had. Is this okay? Is this how God designed it to be? How does this actually serve us?

Having the world at our fingertips can be a good thing in many ways, but when the screen replaces true connection with those around us or we start measuring our worth by how others are presenting themselves on social media, well . . . it can distort our vision. Question: what are you actually doing when you're scrolling through social media? How does it make you feel? Do you feel filled—or hopeless and unworthy? The reality is that social media cannot validate you and, therefore, it can't fill the void that only Jesus can. When we're looking for rest and rejuvenation, that's where Jesus comes in. When we live in Jesus, we are good enough! Not to mention, the "great times" we are reading about from others are highlight reels—highly curated highlight reels.

Are you spending too much time on your phone? If so, maybe take a social media break. You can do this! Instead of scrolling, look up and create a real connection with the person in front of you—or instead of "liking" her last post on Instagram, give your friend a call. We're more connected today than ever before, yet scientists say we feel lonelier than ever. Be reminded in truth today that your worth isn't found in the squares on your Instagram. Your worth is in Jesus! And you are so, so worthy!

YOU GOT THIS!

The next time you're on your phone, take note of how long you're there and what you're doing. What joy is it bringing to your life? Let what you do fill you with joy rather than being part of the comparison game and thinking that you aren't as worthy as others you see. Strive to create an actual connection with friends and family rather than just through social media. How can you change your "phone time" to be beneficial?

CHEERING ON OTHERS

*As you know, we comforted and consoled each of you
as a father soothes his own children, encouraging you to live lives
worthy of God—of the One calling you into His own kingdom
and into His glory.*

I THESSALONIANS 2:11-12 THE VOICE

We each have our time in the sunshine. We can feel unsettled or discouraged about others' successes; even when it's a family member or friend, we tend to wonder when our time will come. Here's a thought: instead of getting down about your circumstances, take it as an opportunity to lift up others! Praise God for the goodness He's doing in their lives. We don't go to God only when things are wrong but also to give Him praise! And not just praise for what He's doing in our lives but also for what He's doing in the lives of others! We often think about "me" when we should think about the "we"—and we tend to think about how to build "our kingdom" when we should think about "God's kingdom." When we celebrate others' wins and lift them up, they will know they are loved and celebrated.

Think about it: when you get a promotion or when something you've been waiting on happens in your life, how do you want others to act? Do you want them to ignore it and wallow in their own lives or take a step back and remove themselves from the conversation to cheer you on? Have you ever shared good news with someone only for them to respond with something greater that has happened in their lives? It's called being one-upped, and it really doesn't feel good, does it?

We don't have to cheer from the sidelines with our friends and family; we can go on the field and lift up the goodness God is working in and through them! We are all given certain gifts, and we can use these gifts to mentor those who are looking to fulfill their God-given purposes. Your encouragement can go a long way. There are so many ways to share your gifts and cheer others onward. What if the whole world stopped seeing celebrating others as a competition and started seeing it as a way to better the entire community? A lot would change, right? Let's let that change start with us.

YOU GOT THIS! *How do you feel when someone has good news? What if it's something that you were waiting on too—how do you react? Instead of feeling as if their success lessens your worth or your circumstance, take yourself out of the equation and let the other person have their time to shine. Be authentically happy, cheering them on, witnessing the goodness God is doing. Remember, everything is in God's timing, not ours. Be a positive influence in others' lives.*

HIS TIMING
IS PERFECT

For everything there is a season,
and a time for every matter under heaven.

ECCLESIASTES 3:1 ESV

Waiting is really hard, isn't it? Sometimes we wonder how long a season in our life will last. Maybe we want time to just slow down . . . or maybe we want time to speed up and get to the next chapter. Perhaps we're stuck in the in-between, waiting on answers and feeling unsure of which road to take. Or maybe we're wishing that something had already happened.

The good news is that God's timing is perfect. When we start doubting ourselves, He never doubts us—nope, He's always on our side. Jesus has us go through highs and lows, different jobs, and different people in and out of our lives in the most perfect timing. By trusting God, you will see that what He has in store for you is so much more than anything you can imagine. Think of a time when someone or something entered your life at just the right time—a friend, a job, a relationship. . . . God is always working in our lives. If you're feeling stuck, pray. There is a reason you are in this role at this time—try to soak in all the knowledge you can from it! What you are learning right now is important for your future. God is building a masterpiece, and you are a piece in that story. Things may not always be pretty where we see it, but He's working in and through all things. Lean into God with all your heart, mind, and soul as you wait on things to come.

YOU GOT THIS!

Where are you today? Are you uncertain of how it all will fit together? Are you waiting to hear God's next steps for your life? Waiting is hard. And it may take years to hear an answer. Soak up all you can where you are. If you're in a job you hate, learn as much as you can and do the best you can while you're there. No matter your situation, bring it to God, listen to His answer, and obey the direction He leads you.

EQUIPPED

You can make many plans,
but the LORD's purpose will prevail.

PROVERBS 19:21 NLT

You are special. In fact, God created you for many wonderful purposes in life. He is equipping you today to fulfill the amazing plans He has for you! Have you ever felt like God was calling you to do something that you weren't capable of? Or that you weren't ready for? Doubt sets in and you think there's just no way. Unfortunately, too many of us allow doubt to stop us from exploring the treasures God has in store for us and those amazing opportunities go untouched.

When we tell God no, we miss out on so much. Sometimes we don't even realize God was nudging us and we simply think it's a step we're not prepared to take. In fact, when we feel we can't do things and say no instead, we often are left feeling as if God isn't there. We wonder where God is. We wait for God to reveal His plans for us. In fact, God was moving and He was there all along. His plans were just different than ours or came at a different time.

Instead of feeling unequipped, the next time you feel a nudge, ask God if this is from Him and then listen, submit, and obey what you are being called to do, no matter how uneasy it makes you feel. Yes, it can be hard and it can take time. But God is good and He's already laid a path before you. It's up to you to take action.

YOU GOT THIS! *If you feel like you missed the bus on God's plans for you, the good news is, He already knew how you would react. The next time you are being called to an area, don't let the doubt set in. Know your worth and remember that God has already equipped you. You may not know how to do what He wants you to, but a path will be laid before you; people, places, and actions will bring you to where you need to be. It's just up to you to obey and take action.*

YOU GOT THIS

And we know that for those who love God all things work together
for good, for those who are called according to his purpose.

ROMANS 8:28 ESV

Throughout this book, I hope you were encouraged to make positive changes to your life and work. When we make the decision to commit ourselves to Jesus—mind, heart, and will—our lives will begin to change for the better. We need to remind ourselves that He died for our sins and accepts us just the way we are! His love is beyond measure. When we accept Jesus into our heart and surrender our life to Him, we are asking Him to work in us. We are asking Him to guide us each day, as twists and turns happen, big and small things, and the great purposes for our life. Today, I challenge you to be all in! Draw near to Jesus!

As you walk your journey with Jesus by your side, your story will come alive, and it will help draw those around you to His light. Don't be afraid to share your story. Shout it from the rooftops—let it stand as a beautiful testimony to God's love for you.

As you live each day, ask God to open opportunities for you to share His love with others. Remember, you are no better than anyone else, and no one is any better than you. Even on the days when the sun doesn't shine upon you, look for peace and joy in those times rather than living in the shadows. Don't forget to listen for the good and reject the bad. There is no doubt that evil forces will try to bring you down, but your God is bigger than any force that comes against you. Know that you have purpose, even if the plans haven't been revealed to you yet. And keep your head up. Be strong and courageous in everything you set out to do. When you're faced with challenges, remember to put on the armor of God. And above all else, just know, you got this!

YOU GOT THIS! *God is working in your life— He always has and always will. Never feel like you can't do something if you know you're being called to do it. His plans for you are mighty and good. Always stay humble and kind and give credit to the One who is working to make all things good. When you feel the need of guidance, open your Bible or look back on this devotional. I hope it will serve you for years to come! Thank you for taking this journey to equip and empower yourself. Know you got this!*

work hard
stay humble
be kind
take the leap

DaySpring

LIVE YOUR FAITH

Dear Friend,

This book was prayerfully crafted with you, the reader, in mind—every word, every sentence, every page—was thoughtfully written, designed, and packaged to encourage you...right where you are this very moment. At DaySpring, our vision is to see every person experience the life-changing message of God's love. So, as we worked through rough drafts, design changes, edits and details, we prayed for you to deeply experience His unfailing love, indescribable peace, and pure joy. It is our sincere hope that through these Truth-filled pages your heart will be blessed, knowing that God cares about you—your desires and disappointments, your challenges and dreams.

He knows. He cares. He loves you unconditionally.

BLESSINGS!
THE DAYSPRING BOOK TEAM

**Additional copies of this book and
other DaySpring titles can be purchased
at fine retailers everywhere.
Order online at dayspring.com
or
by phone at 1-877-751-4347**